DOGS

DOGS

DR. BRUCE FOGLE

A Dorling Kindersley Book

Dorling Kindersley

LONDON • NEW YORK • SYDNEY • DELHI • PARIS • MUNICH • JOHANNESBURG

PROJECT EDITOR Jill Fornary
ART EDITOR Helen Diplock
DTP DESIGNER Sonia Charbonnier
MANAGING EDITOR Sharon Lucas
MANAGING ART EDITOR Derek Coombes

First published in Great Britain by Dorling Kindersley Limited
9 Henrietta Street, Covent Garden, London WC2E 8PS

A CIP catalogue record for this book is available from the British Library

ISBN 0-7513-0856-0

Reproduced by Colourscan, Singapore
Printed and bound by L.E.G.O., Italy

For our complete catalogue visit
www.dk.com

CONTENTS

SELECTIVE BREEDING

THE WIDE VARIETY AMONG dog breeds reflects the judgments of highly skilled breeders. Characteristics such as reduced or enhanced size, speed, scent following, herd guarding, sociability, and dependence were selected for at least 5,000 years ago. Later, "arrested" behaviours such as pointing, setting, and retrieving led to new roles for dogs. Today, most dogs are bred to kennel club rather than working standards, and often do not resemble even recent ancestors.

FORM AND BEHAVIOUR

In ancient societies, dogs were bred for utilitarian purposes – watchdog barking, or defending territory or livestock from predators. With no understanding of genetic science, dog breeders accentuated certain behaviours and body forms by breeding dogs that shared these features. Breeding a large male to a large female enhanced size; breeding two dogs that alarm-barked improved watchdog skill. By selectively breeding for a specific function, "types" began to emerge – Nordic and high-mountain dogs with dense, insulating coats; Middle Eastern, North African, Indian, and Southeast Asian breeds with short coats that

Bloodhound

**Cardigan
Welsh Corgi**

retain very little heat. Variations to suit climate and terrain, and those imposed by selective breeding, produced groups of dogs similar in looks and abilities. Royalty, who hunted for pleasure, took pride in their hunting dogs and bred them for appearance as well as hunting ability and temperament. Wealthy land owners and aristocrats followed this fashion, and many women of the imperial courts, especially in China, Japan, France, Spain, and Italy, kept small dogs as companions. These were bred for their coat texture, colour, size, and affectionate personalities.

THE ROLE OF KENNEL CLUBS

By the mid-1800s, ownership of selectively bred dogs was common among the affluent throughout Europe. At the first dog shows, a range of vaguely defined "breeds" were exhibited. In 1873, a kennel club was formed in Great Britain, producing a stud book containing the pedigrees of over 4,000 dogs, classified into 40 breeds. Within the next few years, kennel clubs were formed in many other countries. All decreed that dogs must be registered before being exhibited at a show held under kennel club rules. This regulation had a huge influence on the future development of dog breeds, in defining a breed as a group of dogs recognized by a kennel club. To conform to the accepted breed standards, show dogs were often selectively bred to emphasize certain characteristics that no longer served any working function. For example, the Bulldog has a prominent head, useful in its original role of baiting bulls. To win at shows, Bulldogs were bred with increasingly large heads, until they became so large that many Bulldogs had to be born by Caesarean section. Other breeds were bred to meet standards for coat length or texture. Thus the Afghan Hound, once an independent mountain dog, today has a luxurious coat, but no longer has the instinct to course gazelles or hunt wolves.

SENSIBLE BREEDING

Breeding away from a dog's origins can accentuate features such as short noses, excessive facial folds, or short, crooked legs. If left to nature, traits that interfere with a dog's vigour and ability to survive on its own are gradually eliminated, since they reduce the animal's ability to compete with more robust creatures. However, what nature determines to be a fault, man may label "desirable". Breeding dogs to comply with breed standards that lead to disease or discomfort is inhumane, and such standards should be modified. Today, many breeders are highly knowledgable in the genetics of breeding, and work to reduce the prevalence of known disorders through selective breeding of specimens that do not carry inherited diseases. Breed clubs also assist by reviewing standards in order to eliminate any worrying characteristics within a breed.

Cairn Terrier

HOW THE BREED ENTRIES WORK

By the late 1800s, kennel clubs and canine societies had been formed, each with its own method of classifying and grouping dog breeds. To rationalize these differences, several European organizations formed the International Cynological Federation (FCI). Its unique nomenclature divides all breeds into 10 groups and numerous subgroups. Original breed clubs retain the right to define the standards for their own breeds, but all clubs affiliated with the FCI submit their standards to that body for international recognition. Since interpretations of standards can vary, some breeds have developed distinctly different looks in different countries. This book follows FCI standards as the norm, but geographical variations are also included. Because the FCI classification is complex, a streamlined method is used, based on breed origins, physical characteristics, and behaviour. The eight categories – primitive dogs, sight hounds, scent hounds, spitz-type dogs, terriers, gundogs, livestock dogs, and companion dogs – are arbitrary. Some breeds, especially crosses between one type and another, could just as accurately be listed in different groups.

28 SIGHT HOUNDS

GREYHOUND

Capable of reaching 60 km/h (37 mph), the elegant Greyhound is the dog world's most important speed merchant. This surprisingly gentle breed uses speed and sight to overtake prey, be it a living animal in the field or desert, or a mechanical rabbit on a dog track. The pet Greyhound is a delightful and relaxed companion, although dogs that have retired from racing have a tendency to chase anything that moves.

Fine, close hair on long, arched, muscular neck

KEY FACTS

COUNTRY OF ORIGIN Egypt/Great Britain
DATE OF ORIGIN Antiquity
FIRST USE Large-game coursing
USE TODAY Racing, coursing, companion
LIFE EXPECTANCY 10–12 years
WEIGHT RANGE 27–32 kg (60–70 lb)
HEIGHT RANGE 69–76 cm (27–30 in)

WHITE FAWN

RED RED BRINDLE

BLACK BRINDLE BLACK

Key facts about breed, including origins, uses, lifespan, other names, weight, and height (at the highest point of the shoulders, behind the neck)

Description of breed's coat colours

*Annotated
photograph
of head*

*History of origins,
development, and
uses of breed*

*Commonly used breed
name, followed by
information on breed's
form, function, history,
and behaviour*

GREYHOUND 29

BREED HISTORY A 4,900-year-
old carving on an Egyptian
tomb confirms the antiquity
of this breed. Exported
to Spain, China, Persia,
and elsewhere, the
Greyhound was developed
to its present form in Great
Britain. Its name derives from
the old Saxon word *grei*,
meaning fine, or beautiful.

*Face is long and
moderately wide,
with flat skull*

160 TERRIERS

SCOTTISH TERRIER

This solid, quiet, and even dour dog has always
been more popular in North America than in
Great Britain. The American president Franklin
Delano Roosevelt often travelled
with his Scottie, Fala, and Walt
Disney perpetuated the
gentlemanly image of this
breed in his film, *Lady
and the Tramp*. Primarily
a companion, the Scottie
is reserved and a little
aloof, and makes an
excellent guardian.

SCOTTISH TERRIER 161

BREED HISTORY The Scottie of
today is probably a descendant
of dogs from the Scottish Western
Isles, which were selectively bred
in Aberdeen in the mid-1800s.

WHEATEN RED
BRINDLE

BLACK BLACK
BRINDLE

*Very sturdy,
muscular
build*

*Tapering tail
is carried up*

*Hindquarters
are extremely
powerful*

KEY FACTS
COUNTRY OF ORIGIN Great Britain
DATE OF ORIGIN 1800s
FIRST USE Small-mammal hunting
USE TODAY Companion
LIFE EXPECTANCY 13–14 years
OTHER NAME Aberdeen Terrier
WEIGHT RANGE 8.5–10.5 kg (19–23 lb)
HEIGHT RANGE 25–28 cm (10–11 in)

*Eyebrows
are long and
distinctive*

*Harsh, thick topcoat,
with soft undercoat*

*Symbols highlighting
breed characteristics
(explained on book flap)*

*Annotations
describing details
of breed's anatomy
and conformation*

*Healthy
representative
of breed*

KEY TO THE COAT COLOUR BOXES

Coat colours are so rich and varied that one word is often insufficient to describe what the eye sees. Each box shown in the book represents a group of colours. The accompanying label specifies the coat colours in which the breed occurs, space permitting. As an example, RED, TAN means red or tan, BLACK/TAN means black and tan, and YELLOW-RED means yellowish red. Listed below is the range of colours that the boxes include; some terms are specific to particular breeds.

VARIETY OF COLOURS, OR ANY COLOUR
Coats that occur in a variety of colours which require more than six colour categories, or coats that occur in any colour

LONG   SHORT

CREAM
Includes white, ivory, blond, lemon, yellow, and sable

GREY
Includes silver, black/silver, silver-fawn, sandy pepper, pepper, grizzle, dark grizzle, slate, blue-black grey, and grey

GOLD
Includes gold, yellow-gold, golden, fawn, apricot, apricot-fawn, wheaten, tawny, tan, yellow-red, straw, mustard, and sandy

LONG   SHORT

RED
Includes red, tawny, tan-red, ruby, rich chestnut, orange, orange-roan, chestnut-roan, rust/orange, and red-gold

LIVER
Includes reddish brown, bronze, and cinnamon shades

BLUE
Includes blue, merle (blue-grey with flecks of black), and speckled blue (with black)

LONG   SHORT   LONG   SHORT

BROWN
Includes mahogany, mid-brown, dark brown, grey-brown, blackish brown, chocolate, and dark chocolate

LIVER AND WHITE
A colour often associated with gundog breeds, including combinations such as brown/white and roan

BLACK
Includes dull black, nearly black, and breeds with pure-black coats that may become grey around the muzzle with age

TAN AND WHITE
A colour combination seen in many breeds of hound

BLACK AND TAN
Clearly defined colours that result in good contrast; includes black/red and black/chestnut

BLACK AND WHITE
Includes black or brindle markings with white, pied, and harlequin

BLUE, MOTTLED WITH TAN
Includes blue and brindle, and bluish black and tan

BLACK, TAN, AND WHITE
Otherwise known as tricolour

LIVER AND TAN
A combination of two reddish shades

RED BRINDLE
Includes orange or mahogany brindle, and dark-fawn brindle

GOLD AND WHITE
Includes white with lemon, gold, or orange spots, and fawn/white; also called bicolour

BLACK BRINDLE
Includes "pepper and salt" (a black/grey combination), tiger, and brown brindle

CHESTNUT, RED, AND WHITE
Includes combinations of white with orange, fawn, red, and chestnut; also described as Blenheim

PRIMITIVE DOGS

THE LABEL "PRIMITIVE" is an arbitrary one applied to a small group of dogs that are descended from the Indian Plains Wolf, *Canis lupus pallipes*. Although from the same root stock as dogs like the Dingo, which are genuinely primitive (in that they are at an early or arrested stage of domestication), breeds such as the Mexican Hairless or the Basenji have been dramatically affected by human intervention in their breeding.

FIRST MIGRATIONS

Experts are quite certain that wandering groups of humans spread out of southwest Asia between 10,000 and 15,000 years ago, accompanied by pariah (scavenger) dogs. Dogs had reached the Middle East and North Africa at least 5,000 years ago, through migration and trade (the Phoenicians traded dogs throughout the Mediterranean). Images of the oldest recorded breed, the Pharaoh Hound (venerated in ancient Egypt), grace the tombs of the pharaohs.

EARLY EVOLUTION

Various primitive breeds eventually spread into the heart of Africa. While some migrated westwards, others accompanied people as they journeyed east. Many followed humans as they traversed the land bridge to the Americas, across what are now the Bering Straits. A number of these Asian pariah dogs interbred with North American wolves, but fossil records indicate that unsullied, distinctly Dingo-like dogs spread first to what is now Arizona, in the southwest United States, and then to southeast America, to the present-day states of Georgia and South Carolina.

Canaan Dog

Basenji

The origins of Central and South American dog breeds are less clear. The indigenous dogs of Mexico and Peru may well be hairless descendants of the Asian pariah dogs, transported further south through migration and trade. It is equally likely that they descend more recently from African pariah dogs brought to Central and South America by European traders.

AUSTRALASIAN BREEDS

Spreading down through Southeast Asia, the Dingo arrived in Australia only 4,000 years ago. A parasite that evolved to live off Australian marsupials infests some wild dogs in Asia, suggesting that the Dingo was traded between Australia and Asia, perhaps by seafarers. The oldest dog fossils found in New Guinea are a

Standard Mexican Hairless

mere 2,000 years old. In some tribes in the Pacific region, dogs were highly prized as guardians and companions; in others, they were looked upon with disgust, or regarded simply as food.

NATURAL SELECTION

The evolution of primitive dogs involved, to a certain extent, self-domestication. Ecological pressures naturally selected for small size; with the growing numbers of dogs around human habitation, small dogs needing less food were most likely to survive. Most pariah breeds are reasonably easy to train in obedience. They are always alert, and can be rather aloof. Some remain at an early stage of human intervention, and therefore lack traits that are the result of selective breeding, such as enhanced sight- or scent-hunting ability, physical power, or a friendly, outgoing nature.

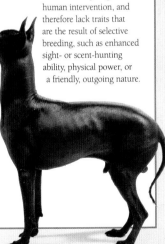

CANAAN DOG

The Canaan Dog used to be employed by the Bedouins as both a herder and guard dog in the Negev desert. Today's breed, which was developed in the 1930s, has proved to be exceptionally versatile. During World War II, a number of Canaans were trained for mine detection; after the war, members of the breed were even used as guide dogs for the blind. The Canaan Dog is now used for herding, guarding, tracking, and search and rescue. Although rather aloof, it does make a good companion.

Bushy tail curls over back when dog is alert

Strong body, with moderately deep chest

KEY FACTS

COUNTRY OF ORIGIN Israel

DATE OF ORIGIN Antiquity

FIRST USE Pariah – scavenger

USE TODAY Livestock guarding, herding, tracking, search and rescue, companion

LIFE EXPECTANCY 12–13 years

OTHER NAME Kelef K'naani

WEIGHT RANGE
16–25 kg (35–55 lb)

HEIGHT RANGE
48–61 cm (19–24 in)

BREED HISTORY Originally a pariah, or scavenger, the Canaan Dog has existed in the Middle East for centuries. In the 1930s, Dr. Rudolphina Menzel, an Israeli authority on dogs, conducted a selective breeding programme in Jerusalem, producing today's resourceful, versatile breed. Increasingly popular, the breed has now spread to the United States.

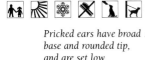

Pricked ears have broad base and rounded tip, and are set low

Eyes are dark and slant very slightly

WHITE

SANDY

BROWN

BLACK

BASENJI

This quiet and graceful dog is typical of the breeds that evolved in temperate and warm climates. Tan colour provides camouflage, and white patches on the fur and a short coat all help with heat tolerance. These factors, as well as the Basenji's silence while tracking game, make it an efficient hunter. Unlike most breeds of dog, the Basenji has just one sex cycle each year rather than two. It rarely barks, but howls in a curious voice not unlike the sound of an Alpine yodeller. Docile with humans, it has a tendency to wander.

Neck is long and muscular

BASENJI FACTS

COUNTRY OF ORIGIN Central Africa
DATE OF ORIGIN Antiquity
FIRST USE Hunting
USE TODAY Companion
LIFE EXPECTANCY 12 years
OTHER NAME Congo Dog
WEIGHT RANGE
9.5–11 kg (21–24 lb)
HEIGHT RANGE
41–43 cm (16–17 in)

BLACK/
WHITE

TAN/
WHITE

BLACK

Long, lean legs allow for free movement

*Pointed ears
are erect, and
highly mobile*

*Wrinkles give
dog surprised
expression*

BREED HISTORY Although its
exact origins are a mystery,
dogs similar to the Basenji are
depicted in Egyptian tombs
from the Fourth Dynasty.
Today's Basenji descends
from dogs that came from
Zaire in the 1930s.

*Tail curls
in a ring*

STANDARD MEXICAN HAIRLESS

How this breed arrived in Mexico will probably remain a mystery. Images of what appear to be hairless dogs appear in ancient Aztec ruins; it is more likely, however, that these are some other indigenous mammals – it seems that the Aztecs at one time "created" naked animals by using a resin to remove the hair from guinea pigs, which then served as food and bed warmers. This alert, lively, and affectionate breed is often compared to both ancient African pariah dogs and European terriers. Its physical structure is reminiscent of classic sight hounds, while its personality can be very similar to the Fox Terrier's. There are Toy and Miniature varieties; the latter is much more common than the Standard.

BREED HISTORY Most references indicate that this hairless breed existed in Mexico at the time of the Spanish Conquest, in the early 1500s. It was probably introduced to Central and South America by Spanish traders.

*Eyes are slightly
almond shaped*

*Head is rather
broad, with
tapering muzzle*

*Deep chest
is fairly
narrow,
descending
as far as
elbows*

*Forelegs are
long and
straight*

ORANGE

SLATE

BLACK

KEY FACTS

COUNTRY OF ORIGIN Mexico

DATE OF ORIGIN Unknown

FIRST USE Companion,
comforter

USE TODAY Companion

LIFE EXPECTANCY 12–15 years

OTHER NAMES Xoloitzcuintli,
Tepeizeuintli

WEIGHT RANGE
9–14 kg (20–31 lb)

HEIGHT RANGE
41–57 cm (16–22½ in)

PHARAOH HOUND

Skeletal remains indicate that hunting dogs similar to the Pharaoh Hound have existed in the Middle East for at least 5,000 years and around the rest of the Mediterranean for about 2,000 years. They survived particularly well as distinct breeds in relatively isolated places such as the Maltese and Balearic islands. The Pharaoh Hound, with its rich, red colour, has become the most popular of these dogs. It hunts by sight, sound, and smell; in contrast, the greyhound hunts by sight alone.

KEY FACTS

COUNTRY OF ORIGIN Malta

DATE OF ORIGIN Antiquity

FIRST USE Sight/scent/sound hound

USE TODAY Companion, hunting

LIFE EXPECTANCY 12–14 years

OTHER NAME Kelb-tal Fenek (Rabbit Dog)

WEIGHT RANGE
20–25 kg (45–55 lb)

HEIGHT RANGE
53–64 cm (12–25 in)

Shoulders are laid well back

Short, glossy, but slightly harsh, coat needs little grooming

White-tipped feet are strong and firm; pads and claws are light in colour

BREED HISTORY The elegant, dignified Pharaoh Hound is probably descended from the small, lithe wolf that once inhabited the Arabian Peninsula. Phoenician traders brought the breed to the islands of Malta and Gozo approximately 2,000 years ago, where it has remained isolated in a pure state.

Long, lean face has chiselled look

Strong and muscular thighs

Tail, which is fairly thick at base and tapers off, is relaxed

IBIZAN HOUND

The coat of the Ibizan Hound can be wiry, smooth, or long, and variously coloured. Although named after Ibiza, one of the Balearic Islands, the breed spread a long time ago to mainland Spain, where it was used both as a gundog, and to course rabbits and hares. Affectionate and even tempered with its owner, it is sometimes sensitive with strangers.

WHITE

FAWN

FAWN/
WHITE

RED

RED/
WHITE

Large ears on long, flat head funnel sounds to assist in hunting

Steep, rather short shoulders above long, straight legs

Flesh-coloured nose pales when dog is unwell

KEY FACTS

COUNTRY OF ORIGIN Balearic Islands

DATE OF ORIGIN Antiquity

FIRST USE Sight/scent/sound hunting

USE TODAY Companion, retrieving, hunting

LIFE EXPECTANCY 12 years

OTHER NAMES Balearic Dog, Ca Eibisenc, Podenco Ibicenco

WEIGHT RANGE
19–25 kg (42–55 lb)

HEIGHT RANGE
56–74 cm (22–29 in)

BREED HISTORY Traders brought the Ibizan Hound to Mediterranean islands thousands of years ago. The breed spread to Mediterranean France, where it was known as the Charnique.

Strong, lean thighs are well suited to bursts of speed

Well-arched toes, with light-coloured claws

Tail is long and low set

SIGHT HOUNDS

BRED FOR SPEED, with an aerodynamic build for flying like arrows after their prey, sight hounds are almost invariably tall, long, lean, lithe running hounds. They are products of highly sophisticated selective breeding thousands of years ago; all emanated from southwest Asia. Some are close relatives of the primitive dogs, such as the Ibizan and Pharaoh Hounds, and the distinction between the two groups is strictly arbitrary.

EARLY BREEDING AND USES

Arabia is the heartland of the oldest recorded sight hounds. Both the Saluki and Sloughi have been selectively bred there for at least 5,000 years, to outrun desert gazelles; in ancient Persia, the streamlined Saluki once existed in 16 different varieties.

Similarly, the Afghan Hound (in several varieties) was originally used in Afghanistan to hunt desert foxes and gazelles by day and to guard the tent at night. Russia's most popular sight hound, the elegant Borzoi, existed in numerous forms in Czarist times.

Italian Greyhound

Breeders are currently looking to recreate many of these lost varieties.

Sight hounds thrived further south, in India, and exist there today, some of them powerful, leggy hounds developed to chase jackals and hares.

Sight hounds were probably introduced into Mediterranean Europe and Africa by Phoenician traders. The greyhound, images of which have been found on ancient Egyptian tombs, was transformed (probably by Spanish breeders) into a miniature sight hound, the Italian Greyhound, to act as a companion.

DEVELOPMENT IN GREAT BRITAIN

The Phoenicians, while trading in tin, may also have transported hounds to Great Britain over 2,500 years ago. Here, they were selectively bred and then crossed with mastiff breeds, producing the muscular and powerful

Irish Wolfhound, which became the sight hound of the nobility. Likewise, the sleek Scottish Deerhound evolved to become the esteemed sight hound of Highland chieftains. The English Greyhound, today's thoroughbred racing king, may have been brought to Great Britain by the Celts, to course hares and foxes. More recently, the Whippet was bred as the working man's sight hound, as was, and still is, the Lurcher. Few sight hound breeds exist outside Asia and Europe.

HUNTING BY SIGHT

Although many sight hounds are now kept solely for companionship, at one time they were all bred to hunt, largely by sight – to detect movement, then to chase, capture, and kill prey. Taboos against dogs in fundamentalist Islamic societies do not apply to sight hounds, probably because the bond between the hunter and his dog predates Islam.

Sight hounds thrive on physical activity, and need regular access to open space. Their temperament is generally benign, but not overly demonstrative. They are quiet, usually reliable with children, and, while some breeds make good watchdogs in their natural forms, pure-bred types are not very territorial. However, all sight hounds have a strong instinct to chase small animals.

Sloughi

Afghan Hound

GREYHOUND

Capable of reaching 60 km/h (37 mph), the elegant Greyhound is the dog world's most important speed merchant. This surprisingly gentle breed uses speed and sight to overtake prey, be it a living animal in the field or desert, or a mechanical rabbit on a dog track. The pet Greyhound is a delightful and relaxed companion, although dogs that have retired from racing have a tendency to chase anything that moves.

Fine, close hair on long, arched, muscular neck

KEY FACTS

COUNTRY OF ORIGIN Egypt/Great Britain

DATE OF ORIGIN Antiquity

FIRST USE Large-game coursing

USE TODAY Racing, coursing, companion

LIFE EXPECTANCY 10–12 years

WEIGHT RANGE
27–32 kg (60–70 lb)

HEIGHT RANGE
69–76 cm (27–30 in)

WHITE

FAWN

RED

RED BRINDLE

BLACK BRINDLE

BLACK

BREED HISTORY A 4,900-year-old carving on an Egyptian tomb confirms the antiquity of this breed. Exported to Spain, China, Persia, and elsewhere, the Greyhound was developed to its present form in Great Britain. Its name derives from the old Saxon word *grei*, meaning fine, or beautiful.

Face is long and moderately wide, with flat skull

Capacious chest provides ample room for heart and lungs

Long, straight forelegs are well boned

ITALIAN GREYHOUND

A perfect miniature, the high-stepping Italian Greyhound has been the companion of pharaohs of Egypt, rulers of the Roman Empire, and kings and queens of Europe. Discerning, a little bashful and retiring in temperament, but still a typically determined and resourceful dog, this sleek breed is an ideal companion for fastidious people. Its smooth, close coat sheds very little hair and produces almost no odour. Relaxed in temperament, the Italian Greyhound is not demanding; however, it does enjoy the comforts of life. Although its refined, thin-boned body is rather delicate, the breed's good nature is an asset in any dog-loving home.

Slender tail is low set

KEY FACTS

COUNTRY OF ORIGIN Italy

DATE OF ORIGIN Antiquity

FIRST USE Companion

USE TODAY Companion

LIFE EXPECTANCY 13–14 years

OTHER NAME Piccolo Levrieri Italiani

WEIGHT RANGE
3–3.5 kg (7–8 lb)

HEIGHT RANGE
33–38 cm (13–15 in)

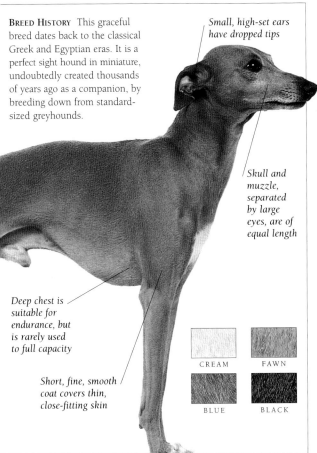

BREED HISTORY This graceful breed dates back to the classical Greek and Egyptian eras. It is a perfect sight hound in miniature, undoubtedly created thousands of years ago as a companion, by breeding down from standard-sized greyhounds.

Small, high-set ears have dropped tips

Skull and muzzle, separated by large eyes, are of equal length

Deep chest is suitable for endurance, but is rarely used to full capacity

Short, fine, smooth coat covers thin, close-fitting skin

CREAM

FAWN

BLUE

BLACK

WHIPPET

The Whippet's aerodynamic body design is ideal for racing – over short distances it is capable of achieving speeds of up to 65 km/h (40 mph). At one time the breed was referred to as the "snap-dog", a possible reference to the snap of a whip. It may look and behave like a delicate breed, and it certainly enjoys the pleasures of curling up on sofas and beds, but in the field its personality changes to that of a robust, fearless, and successful hunter. The breed is gentle and affectionate, and has a good life expectancy. Its coat requires very little grooming, although its thin skin is prone to laceration.

Bright, alert, brown eyes, with quiet, retiring look

ANY COLOUR

KEY FACTS

COUNTRY OF ORIGIN Great Britain

DATE OF ORIGIN 1800s

FIRST USE Coursing, racing

USE TODAY Companion, coursing, racing

LIFE EXPECTANCY 13–14 years

WEIGHT RANGE
12.5–13.5 kg (27–30 lb)

HEIGHT RANGE
43–51 cm (17–20 in)

BREED HISTORY In the 1800s, rabbit coursing was a popular sport in northern England. To improve the acceleration of the terriers used in this sport, good coursing terriers were bred with small greyhounds, producing today's graceful Whippet.

Long, lean head tapers to nose

Legs are well muscled and strongly boned, and covered by very thin skin

LURCHER

Rarely, if ever, seen outside Ireland and Great Britain, and never bred to a specific standard, the Lurcher is still an extremely common dog in its native islands. Historically, it was a cross breed, the result of matings between greyhounds and either collies or terriers. Today, breeding is carried out in a more systematic manner, with Lurcher bred to Lurcher to perpetuate the breed's prowess at rabbit and hare coursing. There are both short- and long-haired varieties. Gentle with people, the Lurcher makes an amenable companion, but it has high-energy demands and is not well suited to city life. It is a natural racer, and will chase and kill any small game.

KEY FACTS

COUNTRY OF ORIGIN Great Britain/Ireland

DATE OF ORIGIN 1600s

FIRST USE Hare/rabbit coursing

USE TODAY Coursing, companion

LIFE EXPECTANCY 13 years

WEIGHT RANGE
27–32 kg (60–70 lb)

HEIGHT RANGE
69–76 cm (27–30 in)

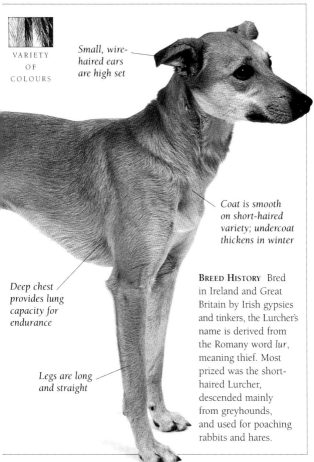

VARIETY
OF
COLOURS

Small, wire-haired ears are high set

Coat is smooth on short-haired variety; undercoat thickens in winter

Deep chest provides lung capacity for endurance

Legs are long and straight

BREED HISTORY Bred in Ireland and Great Britain by Irish gypsies and tinkers, the Lurcher's name is derived from the Romany word *lur*, meaning thief. Most prized was the short-haired Lurcher, descended mainly from greyhounds, and used for poaching rabbits and hares.

DEERHOUND

Ownership of the graceful and gentle Deerhound was once restricted to the Scottish nobility; this is when the breed was developed to course deer through the dense forests of the Scottish Highlands. With the felling of the forests in the early 1700s and the introduction of the gun for hunting, the breed lost its popularity. Today, this dignified hound is most common in South Africa, while in Scotland its numbers are quite small. It is very much like a greyhound in appearance, but with a weather-resistant coat. A good-natured breed, it gets on well with other dogs.

Strong neck is well developed

Feet are compact, with only short hair between toes

KEY FACTS

COUNTRY OF ORIGIN Great Britain

DATE OF ORIGIN Middle Ages

FIRST USE Deer hunting

USE TODAY Companion

LIFE EXPECTANCY 11–12 years

OTHER NAME Scottish Deerhound

WEIGHT RANGE
36–45 kg (80–100 lb)

HEIGHT RANGE
71–76 cm (28–30 in)

Hair on body is harsher and more wiry than hair on belly

BREED HISTORY The recorded history of the wistful-looking Deerhound begins in the Middle Ages, when Scottish chieftains used it for hunting. The collapse of the clan system in 1746 threatened its existence, until it was revived by a local breeder, Duncan McNeil.

FAWN

RED

RED BRINDLE

BLUE-GREY

GREY

BLACK BRINDLE

IRISH WOLFHOUND

Originally used by the Celts to hunt wolves, this majestic dog was probably transported to Ireland by the Romans. In the latter half of the 19th century, the breed was successfully recreated, using stock related to the ancient Wolfhound. Affectionate and loyal, today's Wolfhound makes an excellent companion and an effective guard dog. However, due to its enormous size, it needs a great deal of space and is therefore not ideally suited for city life.

Rough, hardy topcoat is particularly wiry and long over eyes and under jaw

Muscular legs, with sturdy bones

*Thighs are long
and straight, like
a greyhound's*

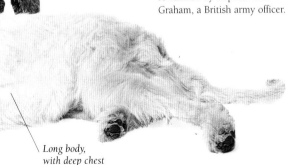

VARIETY
OF
COLOURS

*Long body,
with deep chest*

KEY FACTS

COUNTRY OF ORIGIN Ireland

DATE OF ORIGIN Antiquity/1800s

FIRST USE Wolf hunting

USE TODAY Companion

LIFE EXPECTANCY 11 years

WEIGHT RANGE
40–55 kg (90–120 lb)

HEIGHT RANGE
71–90 cm (28–35 in)

BREED HISTORY Present in
Ireland almost 2,000 years ago,
this noble breed had almost
completely vanished by the
mid-1800s, when it was
revitalized by Captain G.A.
Graham, a British army officer.

BORZOI

In Russia, *borzoi* is a general term for sight hounds, with the Tasy, Taigan, South Russian Steppe Hound, and Chortai (from various former Soviet republics and Russia) all being classified as borzois. The size, speed, strength, and symmetry of this breed made it a superb hunter. Wolf coursing was at one time popular among the Russian aristocracy. The Borzoi could outrun most wolves – working in pairs, the dogs would grab their prey behind the ears, and hold it to the ground. For almost a century, the breed has been bred outside Russia strictly for companionship. In losing its interest and aptitude for hunting, it has become a gentle and amenable companion for people of all ages.

ANY
COLOUR

Long and hare-like feet are covered in short, flat hair

KEY FACTS

COUNTRY OF ORIGIN Russia

DATE OF ORIGIN Middle Ages

FIRST USE Wolf hunting

USE TODAY Companion

LIFE EXPECTANCY 11–13 years

OTHER NAME Russian Wolfhound

WEIGHT RANGE
35–48 kg (75–105 lb)

HEIGHT RANGE
69–79 cm (27–31 in)

BREED HISTORY Originally developed to protect its Russian masters from local wolves, the Borzoi is probably descended from the Saluki, Greyhound, and a lean variety of Russian sheepdog.

Oblong eyes are set quite close together

Shoulders are close to body

AFGHAN HOUND

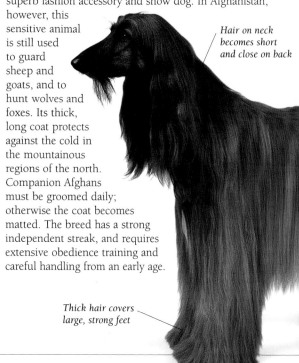

At speed, there is no other breed with the beauty, grace, elegance, and dignity of the Afghan Hound. Developed in the West wholly for looks rather than function, it is a superb fashion accessory and show dog. In Afghanistan, however, this sensitive animal is still used to guard sheep and goats, and to hunt wolves and foxes. Its thick, long coat protects against the cold in the mountainous regions of the north. Companion Afghans must be groomed daily; otherwise the coat becomes matted. The breed has a strong independent streak, and requires extensive obedience training and careful handling from an early age.

Hair on neck becomes short and close on back

Thick hair covers large, strong feet

BREED HISTORY It is not clear how this breed made its way from the Middle East to Afghanistan. There, it exists in three varieties: short-haired like the Kirghiz Taigan (from north of Afghanistan), fringe-haired like the Saluki, and long- and thick-haired, like the true mountain dog first seen in the West in 1907.

Long hair on chest has very fine texture

ANY COLOUR

Tail is set low

KEY FACTS

COUNTRY OF ORIGIN Afghanistan

DATE OF ORIGIN Antiquity/1600s

FIRST USE Large-game hunting

USE TODAY Companion, guarding, hunting

LIFE EXPECTANCY 12–14 years

OTHER NAMES Tazi, Baluchi Hound

WEIGHT RANGE
23–27 kg (50–60 lb)

HEIGHT RANGE
64–74 cm (25–29 in)

SALUKI

According to fundamentalist Islam, dogs are unclean. Special dispensation was given to Salukis, permitting them to live in the home of a true believer. When the Bedouins hunted, they used trained hawks to swoop on prey to slow it down until the Saluki caught up and trapped it for the hunter. Originally the Saluki was carried to the hunt on camels to protect its feet from the burning sand. Today, it is more likely to be taken to hunts in vehicles.

KEY FACTS

COUNTRY OF ORIGIN Middle East

DATE OF ORIGIN Antiquity

FIRST USE Gazelle hunting

USE TODAY Companion, hare coursing

LIFE EXPECTANCY 12 years

OTHER NAMES Arabian Hound, Gazelle Hound, Persian Greyhound

WEIGHT RANGE
14–25 kg (31–55 lb)

HEIGHT RANGE
58–71 cm (22–28 in)

Ears have very long hair

Leg muscles less developed than a greyhound's

WHITE,
CREAM

RED,
GOLDEN

BLACK/
TAN

FAWN

TRICOLOUR

BREED HISTORY The Saluki, which closely resembles dogs depicted on the tombs of Egyptian pharaohs, was the hunting companion of nomadic Bedouin tribesmen. It is possible that the Saluki has been selectively bred for longer than any other breed of dog.

Long, lean, straight bones covered by thin skin

Deep chest built for stamina

SLOUGHI

Like the Saluki, the Sloughi was treated as a member of the family in its native lands, and was mourned for when it died. This breed is very similar in shape and behaviour to the Saluki but has a smooth, close coat. Its range of sand and fawn colours provided an ideal camouflage for hunting desert animals such as gazelles, hares, and Fennec Foxes. Being naturally vigilant, the Sloughi may behave aggressively with strangers. It is not ideal in a home with children – its nervous temperament makes it most content in a quiet atmosphere.

Hocks are close to ground, but not abruptly bent

KEY FACTS

COUNTRY OF ORIGIN North Africa

DATE OF ORIGIN Antiquity

FIRST USE Guarding, hunting

USE TODAY Companion

LIFE EXPECTANCY 12 years

OTHER NAMES Arabian Greyhound, Slughi

WEIGHT RANGE
20–27 kg (45–60 lb)

HEIGHT RANGE
61–72 cm (24–28 in)

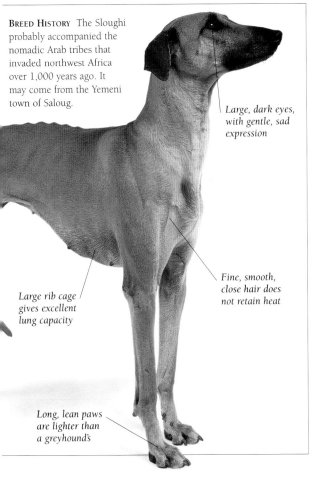

BREED HISTORY The Sloughi probably accompanied the nomadic Arab tribes that invaded northwest Africa over 1,000 years ago. It may come from the Yemeni town of Saloug.

Large, dark eyes, with gentle, sad expression

Fine, smooth, close hair does not retain heat

Large rib cage gives excellent lung capacity

Long, lean paws are lighter than a greyhound's

SCENT HOUNDS

WHILE SIGHT HOUNDS rely on vision and great speed to capture or corner prey, scent hounds use their noses and profound stamina to wear down game and bring it to bay. The Bloodhound, whose nasal membrane has a greater surface area than its entire body, is the supreme scent follower. Where the sight hound chases silently, the scent hound will bark or howl when it encounters the scent trail of its prey.

HUNTING COMPANIONS

No country was more efficient in developing varieties of scent hounds than medieval France. Hundreds of packs of scent hounds, some comprising up to 1,000 dogs, worked the parks and forests of France for the pleasure of the king and his friends. Some scent hounds were smooth haired; others, called griffons, were wire haired. Yet others, known as bassets, were bred with short legs so that hunters could accompany them on foot.

France produced other large hounds, including the Grand Bleu de Gascogne; some are now extremely rare, or even extinct. Smaller hunting dogs, or harriers (taken from the Norman *harier*, to hunt), evolved at the same time, along with basset breeds such as the Basset Bleu de Gascogne, Basset Fauve de Bretagne, and Grand and Petit Basset Griffon Vendéens. British aristocrats routinely acquired French scent hounds; likewise French breeders developed a

American Foxhound

great variety of Anglo-French scent hounds, many of which exist today.

All scent hounds were bred for efficiency in the hunt, not for looks or conformation. It was in Great Britain that the work that began in France reached its greatest sophistication, with the development of breeds such as the Basset Hound, Foxhound, Beagle, Otterhound, and Harrier. Descendants of these dogs were brought to the United States, forming the genetic pool from which the American Foxhound and virtually all the American coonhounds derive.

Grand Basset Griffon Vendéen

using stock from both central Europe and Russia. Scent hounds were the property of the nobility and existed primarily in Europe.

SPECIALIZED SKILLS

In Germany, the dachshund, a dwarfed scent hound (but bred for terrier-like behaviour), was crossed with long-legged scent hounds; breeders also developed cold-trailing hounds that could follow a blood trail days old. Swiss hunters generally accompanied their dogs on foot, so they produced short-legged breeds, while in the Austro-Hungarian Empire, where aristocrats hunted on horseback, long-legged mountain hounds evolved. Norwegian, Swedish, Finnish, and Polish breeders assiduously developed an efficient range of scent hounds,

Grand Bleu de Gascogne

DEDICATED TO WORK

The scenting ability of scent hounds is phenomenal, and they work with staggering intensity. Their drooping, usually long ears create air currents that help them to detect scents, while their pendulous, moist lips can also trap scents. Scent hounds are usually reliable with children and often with other dogs. They are not as demonstrative as terriers, as affectionate as companion dogs, or as trainable as gundogs. Scent hounds are most content when working, be it following the trail of a fox, or the paw prints of the last dog to cross its path.

BLOODHOUND

Throughout the world, breeds such as the American coonhounds, Swiss Jura hounds, Brazilian Mastiff, Bavarian Mountain Hound, and many others trace their lineage back to this ancient scent tracker. Today, all Bloodhounds are black and tan, liver and tan, or red, but in the Middle Ages they occurred in other solid colours. The white variety, which existed in medieval Europe, was called the Talbot Hound. By the 1600s, this strain had died out as a breed, although its genes continue in dogs as diverse as white Boxers and tricoloured Basset Hounds. The Bloodhound thrives on the hunt rather than the kill – it revels in tracking and has been used to hunt animals, criminals, runaway slaves, and lost children. Today, this plodding, sonorously voiced breed is both tracker and companion. Although affable in temperament, it is not easy to obedience train.

Lower lips hang 5 cm (2 in) below jaw bone

BREED HISTORY For centuries, the monks of the St. Hubert monastery in Belgium bred superb, scent-tracking hounds. At the same time, virtually identical hounds were bred in Great Britain. Both breeds had a common source – they may have accompanied crusaders who were returning to Europe from the Middle East.

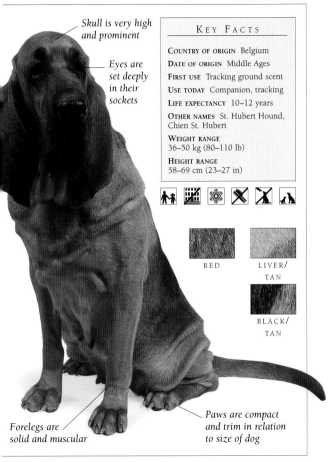

Skull is very high and prominent

Eyes are set deeply in their sockets

KEY FACTS

COUNTRY OF ORIGIN Belgium

DATE OF ORIGIN Middle Ages

FIRST USE Tracking ground scent

USE TODAY Companion, tracking

LIFE EXPECTANCY 10–12 years

OTHER NAMES St. Hubert Hound, Chien St. Hubert

WEIGHT RANGE
36–50 kg (80–110 lb)

HEIGHT RANGE
58–69 cm (23–27 in)

RED

LIVER/
TAN

BLACK/
TAN

Forelegs are solid and muscular

Paws are compact and trim in relation to size of dog

BASSET HOUND

Often stubborn, but usually gentle and benign, the Basset was once a superb hunting dog. Its pendulous ears may have been useful for picking up scent, particularly on damp mornings. Even now, lighter boned Bassets with slightly longer legs and shallower bodies participate in field trials, but the typical pet Basset is heavy, long, and low. Today, the breed is the cartoonist's and advertiser's delight. In the United States, the cartoon character, Fred Basset, personifies droll good humour.

Ears are long and low set

Slightly sunken eyes look soft

BREED HISTORY
The Basset Hound may descend from "dwarfed" bloodhounds. Although the breed originated in France, it is now popular in Great Britain and the United States.

TRICOLOUR   LEMON/ WHITE

Hocks are straight; legs point ahead

Thick tail is carried with slight curve

KEY FACTS

COUNTRY OF ORIGIN France

DATE OF ORIGIN 1500s

FIRST USE Rabbit/hare hunting

USE TODAY Companion, hunting

LIFE EXPECTANCY 12 years

WEIGHT RANGE
18–27 kg (40–60 lb)

HEIGHT RANGE
33–38 cm (13–15 in)

GRAND BLEU DE GASCOGNE

Originating in the hot, dry Midi region of southwest France, this breed is now more numerous in the United States, where it has been bred since the 1700s, than in its country of origin. On both sides of the Atlantic, the elegant and majestic Grand Bleu is used almost solely as a scent-trailing working dog. It is not particularly fast, but has formidable staying power. It declined in numbers when wolves in France became extinct. The Grand Bleus exhibited at French dog shows 100 years ago were predominantly black in colour.

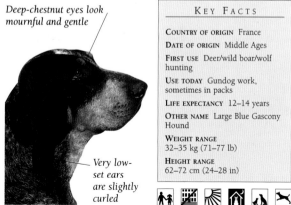

Deep-chestnut eyes look mournful and gentle

Very low-set ears are slightly curled

KEY FACTS

COUNTRY OF ORIGIN France

DATE OF ORIGIN Middle Ages

FIRST USE Deer/wild boar/wolf hunting

USE TODAY Gundog work, sometimes in packs

LIFE EXPECTANCY 12–14 years

OTHER NAME Large Blue Gascony Hound

WEIGHT RANGE
32–35 kg (71–77 lb)

HEIGHT RANGE
62–72 cm (24–28 in)

BREED HISTORY The origins of this ancient dog may lie in racing breeds brought to France by Phoenician traders. It is certainly one of the oldest of hounds whose ancestry cannot be traced.

Oval, wolf-like feet, with lean toes

Well-muscled forelegs support massive shoulders

BASSET BLEU DE GASCOGNE

The Basset Bleu has a good voice and a fine nose, and is an excellent companion and hunter, suitable for either town or countryside. It is not difficult to obedience train, and can make a moderately good watchdog. With its relatively short coat, it is rather sensitive to the cold; some breeders also believe that it is susceptible to gastric torsion, a life-threatening condition in which the stomach twists on itself, usually after a large meal.

KEY FACTS

COUNTRY OF ORIGIN France

DATE OF ORIGIN Middle Ages/ 1800s

FIRST USE Gundog

USE TODAY Companion, gundog

LIFE EXPECTANCY 12–13 years

OTHER NAME Blue Gascony Basset

WEIGHT RANGE
16–18 kg (35–40 lb)

HEIGHT RANGE
34–42 cm (13–16 in)

Long, thin, folded ears are as long as muzzle

Legs are dwarfed to slow dog's running speed

Forehead is long, with slight curve; markings are always symmetrical

BREED HISTORY The breed's origins are lost, and today's Basset Bleu de Gascogne is a recreation of the original breed by the French breeder Alain Bourbon.

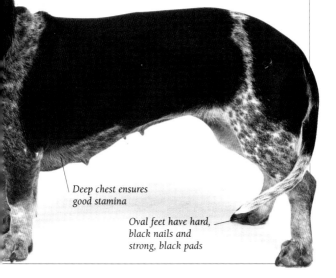

Deep chest ensures good stamina

Oval feet have hard, black nails and strong, black pads

GRAND BASSET GRIFFON VENDÉEN

Taller than most bassets, the Grand Basset is handsome and independent, with a strong will of its own. Although obstinate, it is an affectionate breed, with a lower-than-average tendency to snap or bite. It enjoys working on its own or in a pack, and with training makes a good rabbit and hare hunter. Content to live in a city environment, the dog's dense coat needs regular grooming.

KEY FACTS

COUNTRY OF ORIGIN France

DATE OF ORIGIN 1800s

FIRST USE Gundog, hare coursing

USE TODAY Companion, gundog

LIFE EXPECTANCY 12 years

OTHER NAME Large Vendéen Griffon Basset

WEIGHT RANGE
18–20 kg (40–44 lb)

HEIGHT RANGE
38–42 cm (15–16 in)

Ears hang to tip of nose when scenting

Straight, lean shoulders, well muscled over heavy bone

WHITE

GREY

TRICOLOUR

TAN/
WHITE

BLACK/
WHITE

BREED HISTORY The breed
was selectively created by
a French breeder, Paul
Desamy. Its bloodline
was established by the
middle of the 1940s.

*Long, robust neck is
thickest at shoulders*

*Trim feet permit
effortless walking*

PETIT BASSET GRIFFON VENDÉEN

The most popular of all the griffon vendéens, the Petit Basset has gained the affection of breeders and owners in many parts of the world, including Great Britain and the United States. Truly basset in shape, this alert, enthusiastic dog has a tendency to suffer from back pain. Males are known to fight among themselves for "top dog" recognition from their human caretakers. The breed prefers brisk, cool weather to sultry, humid heat.

WHITE

TRICOLOUR

ORANGE/ WHITE

KEY FACTS

COUNTRY OF ORIGIN France

DATE OF ORIGIN 1700s

FIRST USE Hare coursing

USE TODAY Companion, gundog

LIFE EXPECTANCY 12 years

OTHER NAME Little Griffon Vendéen Basset

WEIGHT RANGE
14–18 kg (31–40 lb)

HEIGHT RANGE
34–38 cm (13–15 in)

BREED HISTORY The Petit Basset has its ancient origins in the Vendée region of France. In 1947, its characteristics were fixed by Abel Desamy, a French breeder.

Large, dark eyes

Chest is as deep as a Grand Basset's

Short legs are, nevertheless, firm and straight

BASSET FAUVE DE BRETAGNE

A typical basset, with a long body and short legs, the Basset Fauve has neither the smooth coat of the Basset Hound nor the rough, wiry coat of the Griffon Vendéen, but rather a coarse, hard coat. Tenacious and durable, it both scents and flushes game, and is most at home working difficult terrain. Traditionally, this basset hunted in packs of four, but when it works today it is more likely to hunt singly or with a partner. It is a lively, opinionated breed, more difficult to obedience train than the related Griffon Fauve, an ancient hound once used in Brittany for hunting wolves. Although it makes a fine companion, like most dogs, it is unhappy when confined and thrives on physical activity.

KEY FACTS

COUNTRY OF ORIGIN France

DATE OF ORIGIN 1800s

FIRST USE Small-game hunting

USE TODAY Companion, gundog

LIFE EXPECTANCY 12–14 years

OTHER NAME Tawny Brittany Basset

WEIGHT RANGE
16–18 kg (36–40 lb)

HEIGHT RANGE
32–38 cm (13–15 in)

FAWN

RED

Golden hair has harsh texture

Thick tail is not too long

BREED HISTORY Produced by crossing the Griffon Fauve de Bretagne with short-legged hounds from the Vendée region, the Basset Fauve de Bretagne is still rarely seen outside France, except in Great Britain, where it has endeared itself to many breeders.

Ears are set below eye level

Long bones are dwarfed

ENGLISH FOXHOUND

A good voice, a keen nose, a rugged constitution, and an ability to get on with other dogs are all hallmarks of the English Foxhound. The shape and size of individuals once varied across Great Britain. Hounds from Yorkshire were the fastest, while those from Staffordshire were larger and slower, with deeper voices. Today, most English Foxhounds share a similar shape and personality. Although rarely kept as a domestic pet, the breed does make an excellent companion, and its solid voice and attentive nature make it a good guard dog. It is gentle, affectionate, and even tempered, although it can be rather difficult to obedience train. It also has a strong instinct to chase and kill fox-sized animals.

KEY FACTS

COUNTRY OF ORIGIN Great Britain

DATE OF ORIGIN 1400s

FIRST USE Fox hunting

USE TODAY Fox hunting

LIFE EXPECTANCY 11 years

WEIGHT RANGE
25–34 kg (55–75 lb)

HEIGHT RANGE
58–69 cm (23–27 in)

BREED HISTORY In 14th-century Great Britain, fox hunting became popular, creating a demand for speedy dogs. From imported French hounds and native stock, fast, lean hounds eventually evolved.

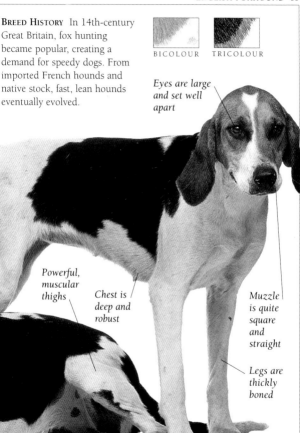

BICOLOUR

TRICOLOUR

Eyes are large and set well apart

Powerful, muscular thighs

Chest is deep and robust

Muzzle is quite square and straight

Legs are thickly boned

HARRIER

Historical records reveal that a pack of British Harriers, the Penistone pack, existed as early as 1260 in southwest England, and that the Harrier was also a popular pack hound in Wales. By the 1900s, however, the breed was near extinction in its country of origin. It was revived through the introduction of foxhound bloodlines – today's Harrier is a successful mix of foxhound and Beagle temperaments. It is at ease with its own kind and bonds well with other dog breeds. The Harrier is also an excellent companion; slightly smaller than a foxhound, its future in Europe and North America is likely to be in the home rather than in the pack.

Upper lips overhang lower jaw

Feet are compact

BREED HISTORY The Harrier was developed in southwest England at least 800 years ago, and probably descends from the Bloodhound crossed with ancestors of today's Beagle. Its name derives from the Norman French word *harier*, which means hunting dog. Today, this breed is secure in both Great Britain and the United States.

Smooth coat is short and flat

VARIETY
OF
COLOURS

Expressive head is not quite as broad as that of a Beagle

KEY FACTS

COUNTRY OF ORIGIN Great Britain

DATE OF ORIGIN Middle Ages

FIRST USE Hare hunting

USE TODAY Hare/fox hunting, companion

LIFE EXPECTANCY 11–12 years

WEIGHT RANGE
22–27 kg (48–60 lb)

HEIGHT RANGE
46–56 cm (18–22 in)

OTTERHOUND

Great Britain produced different hounds for different game, such as the Foxhound for foxes, the Harrier for hares, and the Bloodhound for boars. The Otterhound was created to enter the coldest river and follow an otter to its den. Now that otters are no longer regarded as pests, the Otterhound's original function no longer applies. Fortunately, it has a cheerful disposition, enjoys human companionship, and is reasonably good with children and with other animals. The breed can, however, be stubbornly independent, especially when it sees or smells water.

KEY FACTS

COUNTRY OF ORIGIN Great Britain
DATE OF ORIGIN Antiquity
FIRST USE Otter hunting
USE TODAY Companion
LIFE EXPECTANCY 12 years
WEIGHT RANGE
30–55 kg (65–120 lb)
HEIGHT RANGE
58–69 cm (23–27 in)

Well-muscled
hindquarters

ANY
HOUND
COLOUR

Back is long, strong, slightly arched, and covered by dense, insulating double coat

Lips are fairly heavy

Harsh, bristly topcoat covers woolly undercoat

BREED HISTORY The Otterhound might descend from the Bloodhound. Alternatively, it could be a cross between large, rough-coated terriers, ancient foxhounds, and the Griffon Nivernais, a long-legged, rough-coated hound once numerous in central France.

Toes are suitably webbed for efficient swimming

BEAGLE

A lthough the Beagle is independent, with a strong tendency to wander off when distracted, it is a popular companion because of its affectionate nature and low degree of aggression. An endearing trait of this tranquil breed is its rather elegant and harmonious voice. Its actual size and look vary quite significantly from country to country. Some kennel clubs solve this problem by recognizing different varieties of Beagle with different sizes. At one time in Great Britain, mounted hunters carried small Beagles in their saddlebags.

Upper lips are well defined and pendulous

KEY FACTS

COUNTRY OF ORIGIN Great Britain

DATE OF ORIGIN 1300s

FIRST USE Rabbit/hare hunting

USE TODAY Companion, gundog, field trials

LIFE EXPECTANCY 13 years

OTHER NAME English Beagle

WEIGHT RANGE
8–14 kg (18–30 lb)

HEIGHT RANGE
33–41 cm (13–16 in)

ANY
HOUND
COLOUR

BREED HISTORY The Beagle may be descended from the Harrier and ancient English hounds. Small hounds, which were capable of accompanying rabbit hunters on foot, have existed since the 1300s.

Dark at birth, the nose often turns brown-pink

Long, fine-textured ears hang in graceful fold

Head has slightly domed skull

Smooth coat; can also be wiry

Moderately deep chest, with well-sprung ribs

Thighs have excellent propulsive power

Compact but sturdy feet are very well padded

AMERICAN FOXHOUND

The American Foxhound is taller and lighter boned than its European counterpart, although until the 1900s new blood was routinely introduced from Europe. When working, it tends to act individually, rather than in a group, with each dog having a distinct voice and being willing to take the lead. In the northern United States fox hunting follows traditional European patterns – the hunt is by day and the fox is killed. In southern states a hunt may take place day or night, and the fox is not necessarily killed.

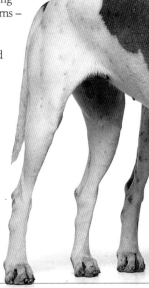

KEY FACTS

COUNTRY OF ORIGIN United States

DATE OF ORIGIN 1800s

FIRST USE Fox hunting

USE TODAY Fox hunting, companion

LIFE EXPECTANCY 11–13 years

WEIGHT RANGE
30–34 kg (65–75 lb)

HEIGHT RANGE
53–64 cm (21–25 in)

ANY
COLOUR

Pendulous upper lips
hang below jaw

Head is
fairly
long, with
moderately
domed skull

BREED HISTORY
The first pack of
working English
Foxhounds arrived
in the United
States from Great
Britain in 1650.
Irish hounds such
as the Kerry Beagle,
brought to America
by Irish emigrants,
and French hounds
helped create
today's lean and
fast breed.

BLACK-AND-TAN COONHOUND

American coonhounds are among the world's most specialized breeds, with a highly developed instinct to follow the scent trail of a raccoon or opossum, and tree the animal. Once the quarry has been cornered, the coonhound remains at the tree, baying until the hunter arrives. The Black-and-tan is the most common coonhound and is assertive, watchful, and obedient. Grooming, with special attention to the ears, and exercise are important.

KEY FACTS

COUNTRY OF ORIGIN United States

DATE OF ORIGIN 1700s

FIRST USE Raccoon hunting

USE TODAY Raccoon hunting

LIFE EXPECTANCY 11–12 years

OTHER NAME American Black-and-tan Coonhound

WEIGHT RANGE
23–34 kg (50–75 lb)

HEIGHT RANGE
58–69 cm (23–27 in)

Ears are set well back and hang gracefully

Long, strong limbs built for prolonged running and swimming

BREED HISTORY Ancestry includes the Bloodhound, Kerry Beagle (an ancient Irish hound), and foxhounds, in particular the Virginia Foxhound of the 1700s. The breed may also be related to the 12th-century Talbot Hound, a white variety of Bloodhound.

Tan colour above eyes

Deep chest for physical endurance

Breed is prone to hip dysplasia, a malformation of the hip joint

PLOTT HOUND

Considered the hardiest of the coonhounds, this large and gregarious dog has been bred by members of the Plott family for almost 250 years, to hunt bears and raccoons in the Appalachian, Blue Ridge, and Great Smoky mountains of the eastern United States. The Plott has a curiously sharp and high-pitched voice, unlike the sonorous bawl common to other coonhounds. Well muscled and rather lean boned, it has the endurance and stamina to work all day and well into the night. It eats large quantities of food quickly, which makes it susceptible to gastric torsion, a life-threatening twisting of the stomach. It is extremely rare outside the southern states, and is seldom kept solely as a companion.

Long tail is held high when dog is alert

Lean, powerful thigh muscles provide energy

KEY FACTS

COUNTRY OF ORIGIN United States

DATE OF ORIGIN 1700s

FIRST USE Bear hunting

USE TODAY Gundog, companion

LIFE EXPECTANCY 12–13 years

WEIGHT RANGE
20–25 kg (45–55 lb)

HEIGHT RANGE
51–61 cm (20–24 in)

BREED HISTORY The only American hound without a British ancestry, its progenitors were German hounds brought to North Carolina in the 1750s by the Plott family.

Ears hang with slight fold

Shoulders are powerful; back slopes from just behind neck to rump

Short coat is thick, dense, and glossy

Deep chest is typical of American coonhounds

BLUE

BLACK BRINDLE

Strong feet have webbed toes

HAMILTONSTÖVARE

Except in Great Britain, where it is fast becoming a successful show dog and working hound, the handsome Hamiltonstövare is virtually unknown outside Scandinavia. One of Sweden's 10 most populous breeds, it is a single rather than a pack hunter, capable of tracking, trailing, and flushing game. It bays in a typical hound-like fashion when it finds wounded quarry. With a coat that thickens considerably in the winter, this industrious dog is content working in snow-covered Swedish forests.

KEY FACTS

COUNTRY OF ORIGIN Sweden

DATE OF ORIGIN 1800s

FIRST USE Game tracking

USE TODAY Companion, gundog

LIFE EXPECTANCY 12–13 years

OTHER NAME Hamilton Hound

WEIGHT RANGE
23–27 kg (50–60 lb)

HEIGHT RANGE
51–61 cm (20–24 in)

Long, powerful neck merges with shoulders

BREED HISTORY Created by Adolf Patrick Hamilton, the founder of the Swedish Kennel Club, by crossing varieties of German Beagle with the English Foxhound and local Swedish hounds, the Hamiltonstövare was first shown in 1886.

Brown eyes have almost serene expression

Strong, dense topcoat covers short, thick, soft undercoat

Tail is thick at root, and tapers to tip

SEGUGIO ITALIANO

The origins of this uniquely attractive breed are revealed through its conformation – it has the long legs of a sight hound and the face of a scent hound. During the Italian Renaissance, the Segugio's beauty made it a highly regarded companion. Today, it is popular as a hunting dog throughout Italy. Its sense of smell is exceptional, and once on the trail of game it is similar to the Bloodhound in its singleminded dedication to the chase. Unlike the Bloodhound, however, the Segugio is also interested in the capture and kill. As both a working dog and a companion, this breed is becoming increasingly popular outside Italy.

KEY FACTS

COUNTRY OF ORIGIN Italy

DATE OF ORIGIN Antiquity

FIRST USE Game hunting

USE TODAY Companion, gundog

LIFE EXPECTANCY 12–13 years

OTHER NAMES Italian Hound, Segugio

WEIGHT RANGE
18–28 kg (40–62 lb)

HEIGHT RANGE
52–58 cm (20½–23 in)

BREED HISTORY
Egyptian artefacts from the time of the pharaohs show that today's Segugio is very similar to the Egyptian coursing hounds of antiquity. Bulk was added to these hounds by introducing mastiff bloodlines.

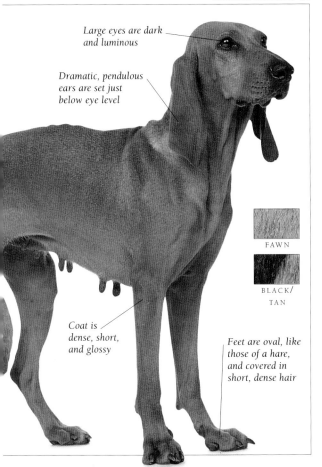

Large eyes are dark and luminous

Dramatic, pendulous ears are set just below eye level

FAWN

BLACK/ TAN

Coat is dense, short, and glossy

Feet are oval, like those of a hare, and covered in short, dense hair

BAVARIAN MOUNTAIN HOUND

Rarely seen, except in the hands of professional foresters and game wardens in Germany and the Czech and Slovak republics, this is a resourceful and ardent cold-scent follower. It usually works independently with its handler, and is frequently used when dogs with inferior blood-scenting ability have lost the trail of a wounded animal; the honour code of the middle European hunter instructs that no animal should be left to die on its own.

FAWN

RED

RED BRINDLE

BLACK BRINDLE

Broad, strong feet, with thick pads and tough nails, enhance agility

BREED HISTORY A small, agile dog with superb scenting ability was required to track wounded deer in the Bavarian mountains. The Hanoverian Hound, a larger German breed, was crossed with short-legged Bavarian hounds to produce such a dog.

Thick, short, hard coat is finest on head

Masked face, with gentle expression and long, drooping ears

Body is powerful and well muscled

KEY FACTS

COUNTRY OF ORIGIN Germany

DATE OF ORIGIN 1800s

FIRST USE Game tracking

USE TODAY Gundog, companion

LIFE EXPECTANCY 12 years

OTHER NAME Bayrischer Gebirgsschweisshund

WEIGHT RANGE
25–35 kg (55–77 lb)

HEIGHT RANGE
50.5–51.5 cm (20 in)

RHODESIAN RIDGEBACK

The standard for this solid dog was created at a meeting of breeders in Bulawayo, Zimbabwe in 1922, when the best attributes of five existing dogs were combined. South African big-game hunters took the breed north, to "lion country", in what was then Rhodesia. Contrary to its nickname and to myth, this muscular dog was never used to attack lions, but acted as a true hound, trailing big game, and then barking to attract the hunter's attention. Its sheer size and brute strength offered protection if it were itself attacked. Loyal and affectionate, few Ridgebacks are worked today; instead they serve as guards and companions.

KEY FACTS

COUNTRY OF ORIGIN South Africa

DATE OF ORIGIN 1800s

FIRST USE Hunting

USE TODAY Companion, security

LIFE EXPECTANCY 12 years

OTHER NAME African Lion Hound

WEIGHT RANGE
30–39 kg (65–85 lb)

HEIGHT RANGE
61–69 cm (24–27 in)

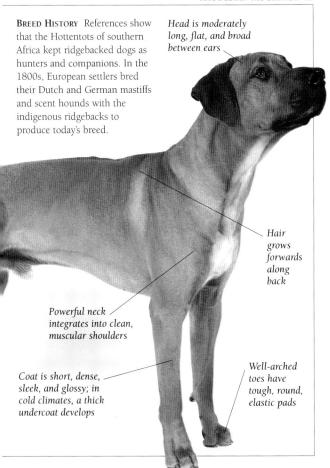

BREED HISTORY References show that the Hottentots of southern Africa kept ridgebacked dogs as hunters and companions. In the 1800s, European settlers bred their Dutch and German mastiffs and scent hounds with the indigenous ridgebacks to produce today's breed.

Head is moderately long, flat, and broad between ears

Hair grows forwards along back

Powerful neck integrates into clean, muscular shoulders

Coat is short, dense, sleek, and glossy; in cold climates, a thick undercoat develops

Well-arched toes have tough, round, elastic pads

SPITZ-TYPE DOGS

No group of dogs has had a more influential relationship with humans than the spitz-type breeds that evolved throughout the Arctic regions of the world, in what are now the Scandinavian countries, and in Russia, Alaska, and Canada. Many tribes of people living in harsh regions along the Arctic seas, across the tundra, and on Arctic islands may not have survived without the help of these versatile canines.

German Spitz

UNCERTAIN ORIGINS

The origin of spitz-type dogs is unclear. No archaeological evidence has been found showing transition stages between the Northern Wolf and the thick-coated, muscular, short-eared, curly-tailed spitz-type breeds. Skeletal remains suggest that it is far more likely that pariah (scavenger) dogs moved north and mated with the larger, more robust wolves of the Arctic. Without doubt, wolf blood has been both intentionally and unintentionally added for at least 5,000 years, producing the wolf-like spitz-type breeds of today.

CANINE MIGRATIONS

Thousands of years ago, descendants of dogs that had moved to the Arctic and interbred with wolves then spread south into the temperate regions of North America, Europe, and Asia. In North America, breeds such as the Alaskan Malamute remained above the Arctic Circle, but in Europe, spitz-type dogs moved south. Bones over 2,000 years old indicate that such breeds have inhabited central Europe for several millennia. These dogs are the likely sources of today's great variety of German spitzen, and of the Dutch Keeshond and Belgian Schipperke. They could also be ancestors of miniaturized breeds such as the Pomeranian. Other spitz-type dogs moved out of northeast Asia into China and Korea, evolving into breeds such as the Chow Chow. Dogs taken to Japan helped found several breeds, including the Akita and Shiba Inu.

VALUABLE WORKERS

The trim, lively spitz-type dogs were initially developed to fulfil three roles: hunting, herding, and draught work pulling sleds. The most powerful and tenacious breeds became big-game hunters. In Scandinavia and Japan, smaller dogs were used to hunt small mammals or birds (and to pull sleds); the Lundehund and Finnish Spitz are their descendants. Draught dogs included the Eskimo Dog, Alaskan Malamute, Samoyed, and Siberian Husky, while in northern Europe and Asia, other breeds were used to herd livestock. Others, with added herding breed bloodlines, were farm workers. More recently, small dogs such as the Pomeranian and Japanese Spitz have been bred solely for companionship.

Alaskan Malamute

PHYSICAL CHARACTERISTICS

The anatomy of spitz-type breeds is well suited to harsh northern climates: a dense, insulating, water-resistant undercoat; small ears to reduce heat loss and the risk of frostbite; and thick fur between the toes to give protection from razor-sharp ice. These dogs have a rugged beauty – their conformation is closest to that of the Northern Wolf, and their natural colours and wedge-shaped muzzles have a distinctly primitive attraction. However, they are not always easy to manage; many breeds require extensive training.

Chow Chow

ALASKAN MALAMUTE

Although wolf-like in appearance, the Alaskan Malamute is an affectionate dog. Not overly demonstrative, it will drop its veneer of dignity and willingly play with people or dogs it knows. This is a powerful dog with a deep chest and outstanding stamina. Although Jack London, in his novels of life in the frozen North, referred to the great strength of huskies, he was probably describing the Malamute. Popular in Canada and the United States as a family companion, the breed thrives on activity and excels in sled-racing competitions.

BREED HISTORY Named after the Mahlemut Inuit living on the Arctic coast of western Alaska, this breed was used as a draught animal long before Europeans visited the Americas.

KEY FACTS

COUNTRY OF ORIGIN United States

DATE OF ORIGIN Antiquity

FIRST USE Sled pulling, hunting

USE TODAY Companion, sled pulling, sled racing

LIFE EXPECTANCY 12 years

WEIGHT RANGE
39–56 kg (85–125 lb)

HEIGHT RANGE
58–71 cm (23–28 in)

Heavily muscled, strong-boned legs are ideal for traction and weight pulling

Females are significantly smaller than males

Almond-shaped eyes are friendly, interested, even mischievous

Small, well-furred ears lose little body heat

Dense coat makes breed prone to heat stroke

ESKIMO DOG

The Eskimo Dog does everything – eating, working, sparring, and arguing – with an abundance of energy. It is independent and requires firm, consistent handling in order to learn to respect its human pack leaders. Eskimo Dogs have strong pack instincts, will readily fight among themselves for seniority, and scavenge food whenever they see it. They also willingly look upon other animals as food. The breed can adapt to living with people and is capable of typical canine affection, but it is most suitable for working.

Expression of dark, well-set eyes is frank and open

Head is neat and wolf-like in appearance

KEY FACTS

COUNTRY OF ORIGIN Canada

DATE OF ORIGIN Antiquity

FIRST USE Backpacking, sled pulling, sled racing

USE TODAY Sled pulling, sled racing

LIFE EXPECTANCY 12–13 years

OTHER NAMES American Husky, Esquimaux

WEIGHT RANGE
27–48 kg (60–105 lb)

HEIGHT RANGE
51–69 cm (20–27 in)

BREED HISTORY For thousands of years, this dog has been the only means of transportation for the Inuit living above Hudson Bay, in what are now the Northwest Territories of Canada. It has remained an aloof, primitive breed.

ANY
COLOUR

Dense coat protects dog from temperatures far below freezing

Tail carried in classic spitz curl

SIBERIAN HUSKY

Smaller and lighter than most other breeds of sled dog, the elegant Siberian Husky is agile, athletic, and a tireless worker. Like other ancient northern spitz types, this breed seldom barks, but engages in communal howling, much like wolves. Very popular in Canada and the United States, the Siberian Husky's coat occurs in a profusion of colours, and it is one of the few breeds that can have blue, brown, hazel, or non-solid-coloured eyes. The breed is dignified and gentle, and makes a very pleasant companion.

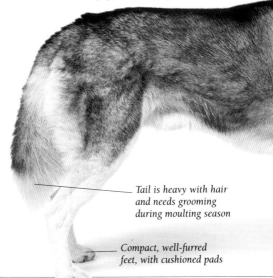

Tail is heavy with hair and needs grooming during moulting season

Compact, well-furred feet, with cushioned pads

Triangular ears are parallel to each other when dog is alert

ANY COLOUR

Unusual patterns like this are unique to the breed

Muscular legs are straight, with substantial bone

BREED HISTORY Used as a draught animal by the nomadic Inuit, the Siberian Husky was chanced upon by 19th-century fur traders and brought to North America in 1909.

KEY FACTS

COUNTRY OF ORIGIN Siberia

DATE OF ORIGIN Antiquity

FIRST USE Sled pulling

USE TODAY Companion, sled racing

LIFE EXPECTANCY 11–13 years

OTHER NAME Arctic Husky

WEIGHT RANGE
16–27 kg (35–60 lb)

HEIGHT RANGE
51–60 cm (20–23½ in)

SAMOYED

Originally a hunter and guardian of reindeer herds, today's snow-white breed retains many of its original traits. The Samoyed is an exceptionally good-natured, friendly dog. It particularly enjoys human companionship, is good with children, and is not aggressive, although it makes a reasonably good watchdog. Like most spitz breeds, the Samoyed does not take readily to obedience training, and obedience classes are advisable. Owners must also be prepared to spend some time regularly grooming the breed's long and luxurious coat.

BREED HISTORY The hardy and adaptable Samoyed accompanied the nomadic tribe of that name for centuries, as it traversed the most northerly regions of Asia. The breed was not introduced into the West until 1889. Breeders have perfected its distinctive coat since then.

Very long and imposing tail

KEY FACTS

COUNTRY OF ORIGIN Russia
DATE OF ORIGIN Antiquity/1600s?
FIRST USE Reindeer herding
USE TODAY Companion
LIFE EXPECTANCY 12 years
OTHER NAME Samoyedskaya
WEIGHT RANGE
23–30 kg (50–66 lb)
HEIGHT RANGE
46–56 cm (18–22 in)

Small ears
are set wide

Deep-set, dark
eyes contrast
with white hair

Ruff of long,
harsh hair
grows through
soft, thick
undercoat

Feet are
large and
rather flat

JAPANESE SPITZ

This rugged little dog is a classic example of miniaturization. It looks remarkably like the Samoyed, yet it is up to five times smaller, and in some ways five times tougher. Lively and bold, the breed was popular in Japan during the 1950s. Although numbers there have declined, it is gaining favour in Europe and North America, as a house protector and guard. It can be an inveterate barker, but breeders have reduced this characteristic.

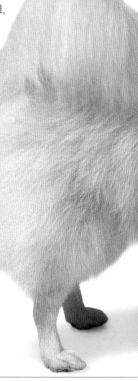

KEY FACTS

COUNTRY OF ORIGIN Japan

DATE OF ORIGIN 1900s

FIRST USE Companion

USE TODAY Companion, security

LIFE EXPECTANCY 12 years

WEIGHT RANGE
5–6 kg (11–13 lb)

HEIGHT RANGE
30–36 cm (12–14 in)

Pointed ears
are erect

Large, oval eyes
are slightly slanted

Small
nose at
end of
wedged-
shaped
face

Dense
feathering
of hair

BREED HISTORY
Everything about the
Japanese Spitz strongly
suggests that it is simply a
small version of the Samoyed.
The nomadic Samoyed tribe
introduced that breed to
Mongolia, from where it could
easily have reached Japan.

JAPANESE AKITA

Japanese breeds are all classified according to their size – large (akita), medium (shika), and small (shiba). Although there are many medium-sized breeds, there is only one large breed, the Akita. This is an impressive dog with a powerful presence. While many individuals are even tempered, some are difficult to handle. By nature the breed is undemonstrative and aloof, which means that obedience training can be irksome. Males, in particular, have a tendency to get into dog fights more frequently than many other breeds. However, well-trained individuals make excellent companions and effective watchdogs. Poised and regal, the Akita is best kept by experienced dog handlers.

KEY FACTS

COUNTRY OF ORIGIN Japan

DATE OF ORIGIN 1600s

FIRST USE Large-game hunting, dog fighting

USE TODAY Companion, security

LIFE EXPECTANCY 10–12 years

OTHER NAMES Akita Inu, Akita

WEIGHT RANGE
34–50 kg (75–110 lb)

HEIGHT RANGE
60–71 cm (24–28 in)

ANY
COLOUR

Stout, strong tail is carried over back when dog is standing

Coat is hard, with fine undercoat

Erect, triangular ears

Rather small eyes are deep brown in colour

BREED HISTORY The Akita, the largest of all Japanese breeds, was once bred for pit fighting. When this sport declined, it was used for hunting. Although by the 1930s numbers had declined to near extinction, the breed's survival was assured by the formation of the Society for the Preservation of Japanese Breeds.

Elbows fit snugly to body

SHIBA INU

Japan's most popular
indigenous dog, the Shiba
Inu is also increasing in
numbers in Australia, Europe,
and North America. At one
time, a tendency towards
poorly developed adult
teeth occurred, but this was
corrected through careful
selective breeding. Like
the Basenji, the Shiba Inu
seldom barks, preferring to
shriek in an extraordinary
manner. Robust and rather
independent, this breed
is a delightful choice for
someone with patience and
dog-handling experience.

*Chest is deep,
with well-
rounded ribs*

*Forelegs are straight,
with elbows held
close to body*

BREED HISTORY The Shiba Inu, the smallest of all the indigenous Japanese breeds, has existed in the Sanin region of Japan for centuries. Bones dating back more than 2,500 years have been found at excavation sites.

VARIETY
OF
COLOURS

Pointed muzzle, with dark nose

Small, triangular eyes

Well-developed legs and thighs support powerful and graceful hips

Thick, strong tail is carried in curl when dog is standing

KEY FACTS

COUNTRY OF ORIGIN Japan

DATE OF ORIGIN Antiquity

FIRST USE Small-game hunting

USE TODAY Companion

LIFE EXPECTANCY 12–13 years

WEIGHT RANGE
8–10 kg (18–22 lb)

HEIGHT RANGE
35–41 cm (14–16 in)

CHOW CHOW

The Chow Chow is probably entitled to be naturally aloof and stubborn. Throughout Mongolia and Manchuria its meat was once a delicacy, and its skin a popular fur for clothing. Its name, however, does not refer to the American cowboy's term for food. In the 1800s, English sailors named it after the term they used to describe miscellaneous ship cargo. Although it looks like an overstuffed teddy bear, the Chow Chow is not cuddly. It is a one-person dog, with a terrier-like tendency to snap or bite. The coat needs intense grooming to remove both undercoat and guard hair (topcoat).

KEY FACTS

COUNTRY OF ORIGIN China

DATE OF ORIGIN Antiquity

FIRST USE Guarding, cart pulling, as food

USE TODAY Companion

LIFE EXPECTANCY 11–12 years

WEIGHT RANGE
20–32 kg (45–70 lb)

HEIGHT RANGE
46–56 cm (18–22 in)

BREED HISTORY The origins of the Chow Chow remain a mystery, although without doubt it is of spitz descent. Historians in the early 1700s described a black-tongued dog being used as food in the Orient. The Chow Chow first arrived in Great Britain in 1780.

Small, dark eyes; tight eyelids often cause medical problems

Tongue is black

RED

FAWN

CREAM, WHITE

BLACK

BLUE

Feet are small and cat-like

FINNISH SPITZ

A hard-working, popular gundog in Finland, this independent, almost cat-like canine has a tremendous voice and is a superb watchdog. In the forest, it listens for wing beats, rushes to the tree where the bird has landed, then barks until the hunter arrives; it hunts squirrels and martens in a similar way. Strong willed, it thrives on exercise, and enjoys working in the coldest weather. This cautious yet lively breed is relatively common in Great Britain and North America, and its popularity is likely to grow.

KEY FACTS

COUNTRY OF ORIGIN Finland

DATE OF ORIGIN Antiquity

FIRST USE Small-mammal hunting

USE TODAY Hunting, companion

LIFE EXPECTANCY 12–14 years

OTHER NAMES Finsk Spets, Suomenpystykorva

WEIGHT RANGE
14–16 kg (31–35 lb)

HEIGHT RANGE
38–51 cm (15–20 in)

Strong forelegs extend from relatively straight shoulders

BREED HISTORY Progenitors of the Finnish Spitz probably accompanied the ancestors of the Finns when they first arrived in Finland. For centuries, this breed inhabited the eastern part of Finland and the Karelian region of Russia. After the Russian Revolution, individuals living in Karelia became known as Karelo-Finnish Laikas.

Tail curves vigorously from root forwards and down

Chest is deep and belly is slightly drawn up

Strong hind legs have small, rounded feet, with insulating hair between toes

FINNISH LAPPHUND

Throughout northern Scandinavia and the Karelian region of Russia, the Sami people used dogs to herd semi-domesticated reindeer. As interest in indigenous breeds of dog developed, both the Swedes and the Finns claimed the Sami reindeer-herding dog as their own. To avoid problems, two breeds were internationally recognized – the Swedish Lapphund, or Lapland Spitz, and the Finnish Lapphund, or Lapinkoira. In Finland, selective breeding ensures that the breed's herding characteristics are not lost. Elsewhere, the Lapphund is more often kept as a companion. Strongly built, it has a dense, luxurious, insulating double coat of hair. Although the breed retains a natural herding instinct, this has diminished through breeding for coat density and colour, rather than for function.

Tail curls over back

Abundant hair is particularly profuse around hindquarters

Well-arched toes

Skull is broad between ears, and slightly domed; ridge above eyes is rather prominent

Short ears are wide at base, erect, and well spaced

BREED HISTORY The historic herding dog of the Sami people, this breed is smaller than the Lapinporokoira, its descendant. The Finnish Lapphund is an example of interbreeding between northern spitz-type dogs and herding dogs from further south in Europe. Originally used to herd reindeer, today it usually herds sheep and cattle.

VARIETY OF COLOURS

Forelegs seem short compared with rest of body

KEY FACTS

COUNTRY OF ORIGIN Finland

DATE OF ORIGIN 1600s

FIRST USE Reindeer herding

USE TODAY Companion, herder

LIFE EXPECTANCY 11–12 years

OTHER NAMES Lapinkoira, Lapland Dog

WEIGHT RANGE
20–21 kg (44–47 lb)

HEIGHT RANGE
46–52 cm (18–20½ in)

SWEDISH LAPPHUND

This is a very old breed, certainly as long established as the lean sight hounds of Asia, which are always portrayed as the most ancient of all dogs. The historic role of the Swedish Lapphund was to herd and guard the Sami people's herds of reindeer against predators. By the 1960s, there was sufficient concern about its guarding ability for the Swedish Kennel Club to undertake a breeding programme to enhance its working capacity. The breed is rarely seen outside its home country, although it can sometimes be found in Finland and Russia.

Hind parts of forelimbs have exceptionally long hair

Belly is only slightly drawn up

BREED HISTORY The 7,000-year-old skeletal remains of a dog found near Varanger in Norway closely resemble today's Lapphund. It is very similar to the Finnish and Russian laikas.

Ears are erect and pointed

LIVER

BLACK

LIVER/ WHITE

BLACK/ WHITE

Short, cone-shaped muzzle narrows to a point at nose

Topcoat is thick and wiry; undercoat is waterproof

Hind legs are very straight

Dense, insulating hair grows between well-arched toes

KEY FACTS

COUNTRY OF ORIGIN Sweden

DATE OF ORIGIN Antiquity/1800s

FIRST USE Reindeer herding

USE TODAY Companion, sheep/ cattle herding

LIFE EXPECTANCY 12–13 years

OTHER NAMES Lapphund, Lapland Spitz, Lapplandska Spets

WEIGHT RANGE
19.5–20.5 kg
(43–45 lb)

HEIGHT RANGE
44–49 cm
(17½–19½ in)

NORWEGIAN BUHUND

The word *bu* means shed or stall in Norwegian, hinting at this breed's original function. The Buhund has a strong herding instinct and thrives on physical activity. It has become increasingly popular in Great Britain, and has been successfully used in Australia as a sheepdog. However, inherited eye and hip problems sometimes occur in the breed. It is an excellent companion, and is good with children. It is also a fine watchdog, and is easy to obedience train.

High-set tail curls over back

KEY FACTS

COUNTRY OF ORIGIN Norway

DATE OF ORIGIN Antiquity

FIRST USE Sheep/cattle herding, farm guarding

USE TODAY Companion, herding, farm guarding

LIFE EXPECTANCY 12–15 years

OTHER NAMES Norsk Buhund, Norwegian Sheepdog

WEIGHT RANGE
24–26 kg (53–58 lb)

HEIGHT RANGE
41–46 cm (16–18 in)

Dark-brown, bright eyes, with dark eyelids

Snout is short

WHEATEN

RED

BLACK

Stocky, compact body

Short, rough topcoat, with dense undercoat

BREED HISTORY The Buhund was originally used to pull sleds and as a hunter's companion. It now serves as both a guard dog and a companion.

NORWEGIAN ELKHOUND

Robust, vigorous, athletic, and with a strong voice, which it willingly uses when it sees its prey, this is the most popular of the three Scandinavian elkhounds. It is the most classic of the spitz breeds, and Stone Age fossils from Norway confirm its antiquity. When working as a gundog it does not chase, but follows its prey in a hound-like manner. An extremely versatile breed, it has been used to hunt lynx and wolves, as well as elks, and is a successful retriever of small game such as rabbits and foxes. Norwegian farmers also use it to herd farmyard chickens and ducks.

Hair is longest on underside of tail, high set with typical spitz curl

Topcoat is thick, abundant, and coarse

BREED HISTORY The national
dog of Norway, this breed has
existed in Scandinavia for at
least 5,000 years. Current
standards were developed
in the late 1800s.

*Small, pointed,
well-furred
ears lose
little heat*

*Muzzle is
tapered, but
not pointed*

*Firm,
muscular
neck*

*Wide, deep, and
well-ribbed chest
is protected by
dense hair*

KEY FACTS

COUNTRY OF ORIGIN Norway

DATE OF ORIGIN Antiquity/1800s

FIRST USE Elk hunting

USE TODAY Companion, gundog

LIFE EXPECTANCY 12–13 years

OTHER NAMES Norsk Elghund
(Gra), Elkhound, Grahund,
Swedish Grey Dog

WEIGHT RANGE
20–23 kg (44–50 lb)

HEIGHT RANGE
49–52 cm (19–21 in)

LUNDEHUND

The small and agile Lundehund is unique in having five, rather than the usual four, supporting toes on its forepaws. The feet themselves have exceptionally large pads, and the fifth digit, or dewclaw, is double in form. This combination gave the dog its superb grip as it climbed cliff pathways and traversed rocky crevasses, until it reached a nest and captured a puffin. Another unique feature is a soft fold across the cartilage of the ear. This unusual anatomical trait enabled the dog to fold down its ears to protect them, presumably from dripping water as it searched through cliff passages for its prey. A lively and responsive breed, the Lundehund is now kept primarily as a companion.

KEY FACTS

COUNTRY OF ORIGIN Norway

DATE OF ORIGIN 1500s

FIRST USE Puffin hunting

USE TODAY Companion

LIFE EXPECTANCY 12 years

OTHER NAME Norwegian Puffin Dog

WEIGHT RANGE
5.5–6.5 kg (12–14 lb)

HEIGHT RANGE
31–39 cm (12–15½ in)

GREY

BLACK

BROWN/
WHITE

BLACK/
WHITE

Moderately muscled hindquarters suitable for agility rather than speed

Medium-sized, erect ears

Brown, fairly deep-set eyes

Dense topcoat lies flat against body

Small, wedge-shaped head

BREED HISTORY
Originating in Vaerog and Rost in northern Norway, for centuries the Lundehund was used to collect puffins from nests on precipitous cliffs. It was not recognized as a distinct breed until 1943.

Extra pad and double dewclaws on forepaws

GERMAN SPITZ

The German Spitz occurs in three varieties of size – giant, standard, and toy. The giant and toy spitzen have always been companion dogs, while the more common standard spitz was once an efficient farm worker. Although the breed has now reached most European countries, its popularity has declined in recent years; even the fiesty and responsive toy variety is losing ground to the Pomeranian, an almost identical breed. This decline is not entirely surprising – spitzen demand more attention than many other breeds; in particular, their coats require routine care to prevent them becoming matted. Unfortunately, many individuals resent grooming, and some, particularly males, resent other dogs or strangers. Unlike many guard dogs, such as the Dobermann and German Shepherd, the German Spitz is not easy to obedience train. However, this refined and confident breed is elegant in the show ring and, when trained, makes an equable companion.

VARIETY
OF
COLOURS

Greatest length of hair is on tail; dense, long, rather harsh hair also covers chest

BREED HISTORY The German Spitz is probably descended from spitz-type herding dogs, which arrived in Europe with Viking plunderers. German literature refers to the spitz as early as 1450. The three types of German Spitz are similar in conformation, only differing in size and colour. The giant spitz occurs in white, brown, or black, while its smaller relatives occur in a wider range of coat colours.

KEY FACTS

COUNTRY OF ORIGIN Germany

DATE OF ORIGIN 1600s

FIRST USE Companion (giant, toy); farm worker (standard)

USE TODAY Companion (giant, standard, toy)

LIFE EXPECTANCY 12–13 years (giant); 13–15 years (standard); 14–15 years (toy)

OTHER NAMES Deutscher Gross Spitz (giant); Deutscher Mittel Spitz (standard); Deutscher Spitz Klein (toy)

WEIGHT RANGE
17.5–18.5 kg (38½–40 lb) – giant;
10.5–11.5 kg (23–41 lb) – standard;
8–10 kg (18–22 lb) – toy

HEIGHT RANGE
40.5–41.5 cm (16 in) – giant;
29–36 cm (11½–14 in) – standard;
23–28 cm (9–11 in) – toy

POMERANIAN

Queen Victoria popularized the Pomeranian when she added some to her kennels. In the early days, the Pomeranian was both larger and whiter than it is now. White was usually associated with a large-sized dog of up to 13 kg (30 lb) in weight, and breeders, selecting for a smaller size, also brought out the now prevalent sable and orange colours. The Pomeranian, being a naturally large breed that has been recently reduced in size, still acts like a "big dog". It will bark unchecked, making it a superb watchdog that will also challenge larger dogs. The breed also makes an excellent companion.

KEY FACTS

COUNTRY OF ORIGIN Germany

DATE OF ORIGIN Middle Ages/1800s

FIRST USE Companion

USE TODAY Companion

LIFE EXPECTANCY 15 years

OTHER NAMES Dwarf Spitz, Loulou

WEIGHT RANGE
2–3 kg (4–5½ lb)

HEIGHT RANGE
22–28 cm (8½–11 in)

CREAM, WHITE, SABLE

RED, ORANGE

BLUE

GREY

BROWN

BLACK

Ears are small and erect, like a fox's

Ruff is typical of all Arctic spitz breeds

BREED HISTORY Today's small dog was developed in Pomerania, Germany, by breeding from small varieties of the German Spitz. Its classic spitz shape and dense coat illustrate its Arctic origins.

Tail lies against side of body

PAPILLON

The dainty looking Papillon is a powder puff in disguise. With dramatic ears reminiscent of a butterfly's wings (*papillon* means butterfly in French), small size, and a fine, silky, and abundant coat, this breed looks like a classic lapdog, content to spend its life watching the world go by. Not so. When trained correctly the Papillon, like the Pomeranian, excels at obedience training. It is a well-constructed, fit breed, suitable for town or countryside. As with most toy breeds, there is a physical tendency to suffer from slipping kneecaps and a psychological tendency to be possessive towards its owner.

Fine, long feet like those of a hare

BREED HISTORY Stories say that the Papillon is descended from the 16th-century Spanish Dwarf Spaniel. Its shape and long coat, however, suggest northern spitz blood in its origins.

KEY FACTS

COUNTRY OF ORIGIN Continental Europe

DATE OF ORIGIN 1600s

FIRST USE Companion

USE TODAY Companion

LIFE EXPECTANCY 13–15 years

OTHER NAME Continental Toy Spaniel

WEIGHT RANGE
4–4.5 kg (9–10 lb)

HEIGHT RANGE
20–28 cm (8–11 in)

Round-tipped ears set towards back of head

Ears carried obliquely, like a butterfly's wings

Abundant, silky topcoat, with no undercoat

Bushy tail requires daily grooming

SCHIPPERKE

The Schipperke may be small, but it retains the personality of a street fighter. This compact package of energy once worked for its living on Flanders and Brabant canal barges, keeping them free from vermin and warning the bargemen of potential intruders. The breed was also used on land, acting as an efficient rat, rabbit, and mole hunter. Resilient and conveniently sized, it makes an ideal household companion.

Muscular and powerful hind legs

Small, round, tight feet

KEY FACTS

COUNTRY OF ORIGIN Belgium

DATE OF ORIGIN Early 1500s

FIRST USE Small-mammal hunting, barge guarding

USE TODAY Companion

LIFE EXPECTANCY 12–13 years

WEIGHT RANGE
3–8 kg (7–18 lb)

HEIGHT RANGE
22–33 cm (9–13 in)

Small, strong, erect ears are set high

Coat is longest around neck

Dark-brown, small, oval eyes

Fox-like head

Dense undercoat makes topcoat stand out, forming ruff

Deep, broad chest, covered with slightly harsh hair

BREED HISTORY This little barge captain's exact origins are unknown, although it has been in existence for many centuries. Anatomically, it is a classic spitz-type dog and is probably related to other continental European spitzen such as the German Spitz and the Pomeranian.

KEESHOND

Although several countries, including the United States, Canada, and Great Britain, classify the Keeshond and the German Wolfspitz (originally used for herding) as separate breeds, in other countries no distinction is made between them. At one time Keeshonds were used as companions on Dutch barges, but they went ashore permanently over 100 years ago. A dapper and sensible breed, the Keeshond makes an excellent watchdog and a good-natured companion, both in towns and in the countryside. It does, however, need firm handling. The breed remains consistently popular in North America.

Feet are very small and cat-like, with thick hair between toes

BREED HISTORY Named after Cornelius (Kees) de Gyselear, a Dutch politician, the Keeshond was once a popular guard and vermin controller in the southern Dutch provinces of Brabant and Limburg. It is the most popular large European spitz in Great Britain and North America.

Hair is tipped with black

Muzzle is not too long and fairly narrow

Profuse coat is densest in ruff around neck

KEY FACTS

COUNTRY OF ORIGIN The Netherlands

DATE OF ORIGIN 1500s

FIRST USE Barge dog

USE TODAY Companion, watchdog

LIFE EXPECTANCY 12–14 years

OTHER NAME Wolfspitz

WEIGHT RANGE
25–30 kg (55–66 lb)

HEIGHT RANGE
43–48 cm (17–19 in)

TERRIERS

Terriers evolved from hounds – the dachshund, which functionally is a terrier-like "earth dog", is a miniaturized, dwarfed scent hound. Through selective breeding, the terrier's aggressive instinct was also enhanced. Expert at tunnelling, these fiesty dogs still willingly engage in head-on combat with burrowing mammals on their opponents' home territories.

Dandie Dinmont Terrier

ANGLO-SAXON ROOTS

Although dachshunds and many other earth dogs evolved in several European countries, most terriers originated in Great Britain. Their name derives from the Latin *terra*, meaning earth. Little reference is made to them until 1560, when renowned British writer Dr. John Caius described them as snappy and quarrelsome. At that time there were only short legged terriers, used solely to bolt down fox and badger holes. While dachshunds had smooth, close coats, these dogs

had rough coats, usually black and tan or mixed fawn, as well as erect ears and sprightly temperaments.

Anything was fair game for these robust, well-muscled dogs – badgers and foxes, but also rats, weasels, ferrets, otters, marmots, mice, and snakes. No working dog was a more efficient killing machine than the tenacious, tunnel-hugging terrier. Going to ground demanded small size, plus an unquestioning fearlessness, resolution, and toughness. These attributes remain today, and explain why terriers are better at overcoming serious illness than any other dog group. Almost nothing interferes with the terrier's zest for life.

EFFICIENT ALL-ROUNDERS

During the 19th century, short-legged terriers, carried in saddlebags, would accompany foxhounds on the hunt.

Yorkshire Terrier

When the hounds cornered their quarry, the terriers were released to inflict the *coup de grâce* upon the fox. Competent and versatile, terriers also rid farm buildings of vermin and were used in sport – as ratters or in fights against dogs or other animals. Bull-baiting breeds were originally large, mastiff-type dogs, but terrier blood was added to heighten their aggression, producing the bull terrier types, which are distinguished from other large, muscular breeds by their tenacity. When they bite, they do not let go. In working breeds such as the Lakeland, Welsh, and Irish Terriers, this is called "gameness". Even show dogs must demonstrate that they are willing to attack a piece of animal hide.

Kerry Blue Terrier

REGIONAL VARIATIONS

Generic, hard-working, short-legged terriers existed throughout Great Britain and Ireland, but in the 1800s breeders began producing regional types, many descended from hunting and retrieving dogs. These breeds do not go to ground but rather chase, capture, kill, and carry. Tough British breeds were also exported elsewhere to create new terriers such as the Czesky.

ENTERTAINING COMPANIONS

As family pets, terriers are a joy. They love rough-and-tumble, have endless energy, and are hugely entertaining. Most terriers make excellent city pets; all retain an instinct to nip, but if excessive yapping is controlled early, they are superb watchdogs and loyal defenders of their realms.

LAKELAND TERRIER

The working Lakeland Terrier was an agile and ruthless hunter, adept at working the rocky ground of Great Britain's Lake District in pursuit of its quarry. It was willing to take on animals far larger than itself. The breed probably descends from extinct black-and-tan terriper stock, from which the Welsh Terrier also originates. The Lakeland has had periods of show-ring popularity, even winning Best in Show in Great Britain and the United States, but in comparison to more fashionable breeds it remains numerically small. It is a single-minded terrier, best suited to owners with patience.

Dark eyes look intent and fearless

WHEATEN

BLUE

RED

BLACK

BLUE/TAN

BLACK/ TAN

BREED HISTORY The fearless and nimble Lakeland Terrier was originally bred and used by farmers in northern England to protect their sheepfolds from predators.

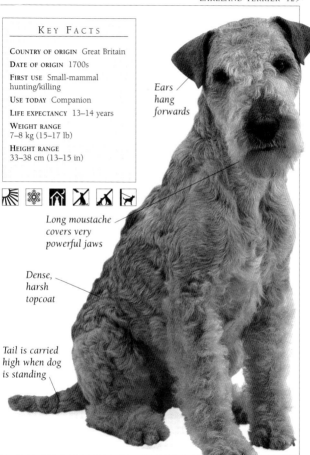

KEY FACTS

COUNTRY OF ORIGIN Great Britain

DATE OF ORIGIN 1700s

FIRST USE Small-mammal hunting/killing

USE TODAY Companion

LIFE EXPECTANCY 13–14 years

WEIGHT RANGE
7–8 kg (15–17 lb)

HEIGHT RANGE
33–38 cm (13–15 in)

Ears hang forwards

Long moustache covers very powerful jaws

Dense, harsh topcoat

Tail is carried high when dog is standing

WELSH TERRIER

This lively and stubborn terrier thrives on mental and physical activity. More popular in North America than in Great Britain, the Welsh Terrier is a compact dog, suitable as a companion but still exceedingly effective as a rural vermin catcher. Coming from a working background, the Welsh Terrier is not very difficult to obedience train, but it does not back down from dog fights.

Strong, muscular thighs and good bone length

KEY FACTS

COUNTRY OF ORIGIN Great Britain

DATE OF ORIGIN 1700s

FIRST USE Ratting

USE TODAY Companion

LIFE EXPECTANCY 14 years

WEIGHT RANGE
9–10 kg (20–22 lb)

HEIGHT RANGE
36–39 cm (14–15½ in)

BREED HISTORY Originating in north Wales in the 1760s, this breed is probably the direct descendant of the previously common but now-extinct black-and-tan Old English Broken- (or Coarse-) haired Terrier.

Small, dark, alert eyes

Slightly arched, thickish neck

Profuse beard catches food and needs routine attention

Abundant, wiry topcoat covers fine undercoat

Small, round feet have hard, black nails and pads

AIREDALE TERRIER

Although the Airedale is far too large to live up to the definition of the word "terrier", which in French means an ability to go to ground, in all other ways it is the essence of this group of dogs. A born watchdog, with a delinquent tendency to get into street brawls with other dogs, the tough, hardy, and faithful Airedale has been used as a police dog, sentry dog, and messenger. Were it not for its inherently strong stubborn streak, it would be a popular and successful working dog.

Beard covers powerful jaws

BREED HISTORY The Airedale Terrier originated in Yorkshire, England, when working men in Leeds crossed the Old English Broken- (or Coarse-) haired Terrier with the Otterhound, producing this extremely versatile "King of Terriers".

KEY FACTS

COUNTRY OF ORIGIN Great Britain

DATE OF ORIGIN 1800s

FIRST USE Badger/otter hunting

USE TODAY Companion, guarding

LIFE EXPECTANCY 13 years

OTHER NAME Waterside Terrier

WEIGHT RANGE
20–23 kg (44–50 lb)

HEIGHT RANGE
56–61 cm (22–24 in)

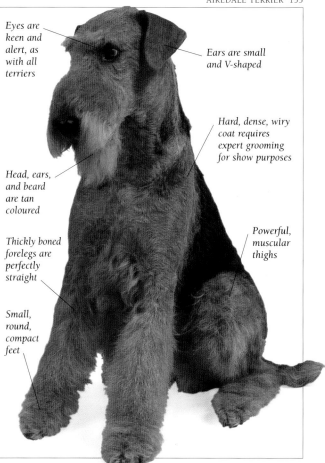

Eyes are keen and alert, as with all terriers

Ears are small and V-shaped

Hard, dense, wiry coat requires expert grooming for show purposes

Head, ears, and beard are tan coloured

Thickly boned forelegs are perfectly straight

Powerful, muscular thighs

Small, round, compact feet

YORKSHIRE TERRIER

This feisty little package of energy is now one of Great Britain's most numerous pure-bred dogs, and is almost equally popular in other parts of Europe and in North America. Many Yorkies are spoiled, and never have the chance to show their willingness to learn. Excessive breeding has also produced nervous and meek examples of the breed, but they are a minority. The typical Yorkshire Terrier is a dynamo, with little understanding of its small size. It plays hard, and has seemingly unlimited energy. Miniaturization has unfortunately brought with it many medical problems, including gum disease and collapsed windpipes. Although often regarded as a fashion accessory, the breed remains true to its origins – tenacious and stubborn.

Ears are V-shaped

BREED HISTORY The world's most popular terrier originated in the early 1800s in the West Riding area of Yorkshire, England. Miners, wanting to develop a ratting terrier small enough to carry in a pocket, probably crossed black-and-tan terriers with the now-extinct Paisley and Clydesdale Terriers.

Deep-black nose may lighten with age

Body hair is long and straight

Long hair can be either brushed to sides or clipped; diligent grooming is essential

Face is very narrow, but bushy whiskers give square look

KEY FACTS

COUNTRY OF ORIGIN Great Britain

DATE OF ORIGIN 1800s

FIRST USE Ratting

USE TODAY Companion

LIFE EXPECTANCY 14 years

WEIGHT RANGE
2.5–3.5 kg (5–7 lb)

HEIGHT RANGE
22.5–23.5 cm (9 in)

AUSTRALIAN SILKY TERRIER

Similar in appearance to, but larger than, the Yorkshire Terrier, the blue-and-tan Australian Silky Terrier successfully colonized the United States and Canada before arriving in Europe. It is a robust breed, yappy like the Yorkie, and just as possessive of its own territory, announcing the presence of strangers in a shrill voice. Although small in size, the Australian Silky is quite capable of killing small rodents. It can become an independent renegade, and early obedience training is necessary if it is to live peacefully with people. A strong-willed breed, it can be intolerant of handling and of strangers, unless it experiences both while quite young. The Silky's coat becomes matted easily and benefits from daily brushing. The breed does not have a dense undercoat, and can suffer in cold climates.

BREED HISTORY The Australian Silky Terrier, developed during the early 1900s, is probably the result of breeding the Australian Terrier with the Yorkshire, and perhaps the Skye Terrier, primarily as a companion.

Powerful, muscular thighs

Tan hair grows from knees down to cat-like feet

KEY FACTS

COUNTRY OF ORIGIN Australia

DATE OF ORIGIN 1900s

FIRST USE Companion

USE TODAY Companion

LIFE EXPECTANCY 14 years

OTHER NAME Silky Terrier

WEIGHT RANGE
4–5 kg (8–11 lb)

HEIGHT RANGE
22.5–23.5 cm (9 in)

Ears are thin,
V-shaped,
and erect

Hair does not
cover eyes

Silver-grey hair
(called blue by
breeders) covers
body and upper legs

AUSTRALIAN TERRIER

Tough and willing to fight anything, the Australian Terrier was an ideal homestead dog. Capable of killing all small vermin, including snakes, it also acted as an alert watchdog, guarding isolated homes from intruders. These traits still exist today – the Australian Terrier is unlikely to back down in confrontations with other dogs, nor is it likely to leave cats in peace, unless it has been raised with them since puppyhood. It makes an entertaining companion, however, and can be trained in obedience. Like the Silky Terrier, it accompanied armed-forces personnel and businessmen to North America after World War II. Although the Australian Terrier is still most popular in Australia and New Zealand, it now exists in all major English-speaking countries.

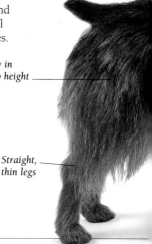

Long body in relation to height

BREED HISTORY This sturdy native of Australia is descended from several British terriers, including the Cairn, Yorkshire, Skye, and perhaps the Norwich. Settlers brought these breeds to Australia in order to produce an efficient ratter to work the farms and ranches.

Straight, thin legs

KEY FACTS

COUNTRY OF ORIGIN Australia

DATE OF ORIGIN 1800s

FIRST USE Farm ratter, watchdog

USE TODAY Companion

LIFE EXPECTANCY 14 years

WEIGHT RANGE
5–6 kg (12–14 lb)

HEIGHT RANGE
24.5–25.5 cm (10 in)

BLUE/TAN

SANDY

Small, dark eyes are vibrant

Long, flat skull

Compact, slightly pursed mouth

Small and compact feet have black nails

IRISH TERRIER

Although now mainly a companion dog, in Ireland the Irish Terrier's hunting abilities are sometimes still put to good use. In the United States, its skills as a water dog and vermin killer have been preserved through field trials and lure coursing. With its striding action and racy lines, this is perhaps the most elegant of terriers. It is a good family playmate, but can be over-boisterous with other dogs, and should be kept on a lead unless obedience trained.

High-set tail is covered with short hair

Hard, wiry topcoat has soft, fine undercoat

KEY FACTS

COUNTRY OF ORIGIN Ireland

DATE OF ORIGIN 1700s

FIRST USE Watchdog, vermin hunting

USE TODAY Companion, field trials, coursing, vermin hunting

LIFE EXPECTANCY 13 years

OTHER NAME Irish Red Terrier

WEIGHT RANGE
11–12 kg (25–27 lb)

HEIGHT RANGE
46–48 cm (18–19 in)

Ears have high
fold and drop
to cheeks

Small, dark eyes
are full of life

Small, neat
beard requires
experienced
clipping

Moderately
long, widening
neck usually
has frills on
each side

BREED HISTORY
Developed in the
districts around Cork,
in southern Ireland,
this sprightly breed is
probably descended
from old black-and-tan
and wheaten terriers.

Straight legs
have plenty of
bone and muscle

KERRY BLUE TERRIER

Kerry Blue puppies are born black, and their coat colour changes to blue between nine and 24 months of age. In general, the earlier the coat changes colour, the lighter it will become. With no undercoat and a non-shedding topcoat, the breed is a good household pet. An all-round terrier, it is an excellent guard, ratter, and water retriever, and is also used for herding and hunting.

KEY FACTS

COUNTRY OF ORIGIN Ireland

DATE OF ORIGIN 1700s

FIRST USE Badger/fox/rat hunting

USE TODAY Companion, field trials, rat/rabbit hunting

LIFE EXPECTANCY 14 years

OTHER NAME Irish Blue Terrier

WEIGHT RANGE
15–17 kg (33–37 lb)

HEIGHT RANGE
46–48 cm (18–19 in)

Profuse beard needs regular grooming

Strong neck runs to sloping shoulders

Small feet covered with dense hair

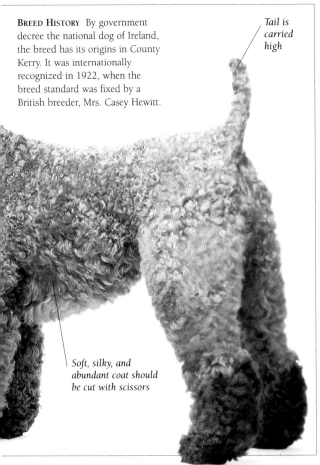

BREED HISTORY By government decree the national dog of Ireland, the breed has its origins in County Kerry. It was internationally recognized in 1922, when the breed standard was fixed by a British breeder, Mrs. Casey Hewitt.

Tail is carried high

Soft, silky, and abundant coat should be cut with scissors

SOFT-COATED WHEATEN TERRIER

Probably the least intense of Ireland's terriers, the Wheaten has recently become a fashionable and enjoyable companion in Canada and the United States. Its rightful popularity is based on a versatility that stems from an ancient Irish law prohibiting peasants from owning hunting dogs. The Wheaten, most definitely "peasant" in appearance, was developed to overcome this restriction. The result is, by terrier standards, a reasonably obedient and trainable companion.

KEY FACTS

COUNTRY OF ORIGIN Ireland

DATE OF ORIGIN 1700s

FIRST USE Herding, vermin hunting

USE TODAY Companion

LIFE EXPECTANCY 13–14 years

WEIGHT RANGE
16–20 kg (35–45 lb)

HEIGHT RANGE
46–48 cm (18–19 in)

BREED HISTORY The Soft-coated
Wheaten Terrier is related to
both the Kerry Blue and Irish
Terriers. Indigenous to the
counties of Kerry and Cork in
southern Ireland, for centuries
it was an all-purpose worker,
used for guarding, droving,
herding, and hunting.

*Head is
fairly long*

*Small, thin,
V-shaped
ears have
fringe of hair*

*Moderately long,
strong neck*

*Wavy, soft coat
has loose curls,
and is colour of
ripening wheat*

*Feet are quite
small and
compact, with
black nails*

GLEN OF IMAAL TERRIER

This is the rarest of Ireland's terriers, and it shares with that island's other "peasant dogs" an intense tenacity of spirit. Before selective breeding improved the Glen's social manners, it was a fierce fox and badger hunter, compact enough to go underground after its quarry and fight it to the death. The breed was used in dog fights, but in contrast to Great Britain, where the fight was staged indoors, in Ireland it took place in open fields. First exhibited in 1933, today's Glen is relatively relaxed, and makes an affectionate companion, although it certainly will not back down from a fight.

Ears hang naturally

Rough, medium-length, tidy topcoat covers insulating, fine undercoat

Slightly turned-out feet, with black nails and firm pads

WHEATEN

BLUE

RED BRINDLE

BLACK BRINDLE

KEY FACTS

COUNTRY OF ORIGIN Ireland

DATE OF ORIGIN 1700s

FIRST USE Vermin hunting

USE TODAY Companion

LIFE EXPECTANCY 13–14 years

WEIGHT RANGE
15.5–16.5 kg (34–36 lb)

HEIGHT RANGE
35.5–36.5 cm (14 in)

BREED HISTORY This ancient breed of unknown origins is named after a valley in County Wicklow, in eastern Ireland. It is tough, sturdy, and adaptable, and was ideal for fox and badger hunting in the rough terrains of the Glen.

Body is longer than it is high, and gives image of sturdy substance

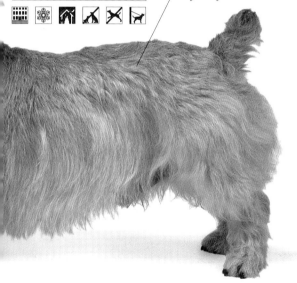

NORFOLK TERRIER

With the exception of the ears, the appearances, origins, personalities, and function of the Norfolk and Norwich Terriers are identical. The Norfolk is a delightful little dog, although it has an instinctive terrier-like desire to attack and throttle any rodent it sees. Like virtually all terriers, it must be introduced to cats carefully, so that its natural instincts can be harnessed. Good natured and robust, the breed makes an excellent companion. It is also a good guard dog, and will bark at strangers or unusual noises. It is happy in either the town or countryside – a back garden provides all the space this short-legged breed needs for vigorous exercise.

KEY FACTS

COUNTRY OF ORIGIN Great Britain

DATE OF ORIGIN 1800s

FIRST USE Ratting

USE TODAY Companion

LIFE EXPECTANCY 14 years

WEIGHT RANGE
5–5.5 kg (11–12 lb)

HEIGHT RANGE
24.5–25.5 cm (9½–10 in)

Small, round feet have firm pads

WHEATEN

RED

BLACK/
TAN

GRIZZLE

*Hard, straight,
and wiry coat*

*Slightly
round-
tipped ears
drop close
to cheeks*

BREED HISTORY
From the time
that it was first
recognized as a
breed, the Norwich
produced puppies with
both erect and drop
ears. The arguments
this created resulted in
the drop-eared Norfolk
being recognized as a
separate breed in 1965.

NORWICH TERRIER

Among the smallest of all terriers, the Norwich has existed in eastern England for over 100 years. In the late 1800s, students at Cambridge University used it as their mascot, but it was not exhibited as a distinct breed until 1935. The Norwich is a typically bossy terrier, which firmly believes in its own importance. It is, however, an ideal family companion, and gets on well with older children. It is less difficult to obedience train than most terriers, and is willing to engage in rigorous exercise. The Norwich is free from most serious inherited medical conditions.

Short, compact body, with wide rib cage

KEY FACTS

COUNTRY OF ORIGIN Great Britain

DATE OF ORIGIN 1800s

FIRST USE Ratting

USE TODAY Companion

LIFE EXPECTANCY 14 years

WEIGHT RANGE
5–5.5 kg (11–12 lb)

HEIGHT RANGE
25–26 cm (10–10½ in)

Head is slightly rounded

Ears are always erect

BREED HISTORY Packs of small, red terriers, which evolved from Irish terriers, existed in the 1800s. The Norwich may be derived from these dogs, or it may be descended from the extinct Trumpington Terrier.

WHEATEN

RED

BLACK/ TAN

GRIZZLE

Thickly muscled hindquarters

BORDER TERRIER

The Border, an uncomplicated and genuine terrier, little altered from its original form, is built to be small enough to follow a fox down the narrowest hole, but with enough leg to keep up with riders on horseback. It has never achieved the show-ring popularity of other terriers, and has therefore remained true to its original form and function. Its durable coat protects it from adverse weather conditions; its long legs and stamina enable it to keep up with the most demanding activity. The Border's amenable personality makes it a superb family dog.

BREED HISTORY The exact origins of this breed are unknown. There is evidence that it existed in the borders between England and Scotland, in much its present form, in the late 1700s.

KEY FACTS

COUNTRY OF ORIGIN Great Britain

DATE OF ORIGIN 1700s

FIRST USE Ratting, worrying foxes from lairs

USE TODAY Companion, hunt follower

LIFE EXPECTANCY 13–14 years

WEIGHT RANGE
5–7 kg (11½–15 lb)

HEIGHT RANGE
25–28 cm (10–11 in)

WHEATEN

TAN-RED

GRIZZLE

BLUE/TAN

Dark eyes look keen and alert

Small, V-shaped ears

Short muzzle

Harsh, dense topcoat

Hind legs have sturdy loins

CAIRN TERRIER

Until recently, when the West Highland White and Yorkshire Terriers superseded it, this was the most popular of all Great Britain's terriers. In the early 1900s, breeders were careful to retain the Cairn's natural shaggy coat, sturdy body, and terrier abilities. The breed is equally at home in town or country. It makes a good watchdog, and is easier to obedience train than many other terriers. The terrier temperament is, however, always there. Males, in particular, can be bossy, and should be monitored when meeting children for the first time. The Cairn's small size, good health, and lack of stubbornness make it a delightful companion.

Forelegs are moderately long —

CREAM

WHEATEN

NEARLY BLACK

GREY

RED

Front feet are larger than back feet

BREED HISTORY The Cairn may have originated on the Scottish Isle of Skye where, since at least the time of Mary Queen of Scots, it worked the cairns, searching for hiding foxes.

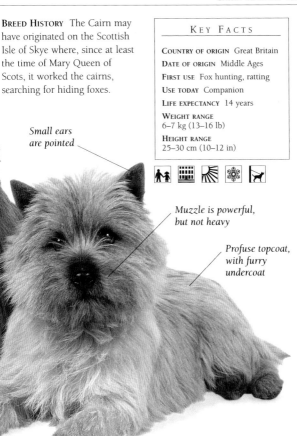

KEY FACTS

COUNTRY OF ORIGIN Great Britain

DATE OF ORIGIN Middle Ages

FIRST USE Fox hunting, ratting

USE TODAY Companion

LIFE EXPECTANCY 14 years

WEIGHT RANGE
6–7 kg (13–16 lb)

HEIGHT RANGE
25–30 cm (10–12 in)

Small ears are pointed

Muzzle is powerful, but not heavy

Profuse topcoat, with furry undercoat

WEST HIGHLAND WHITE TERRIER

Although the West Highland White and Cairn Terriers share a common ancestry, selective breeding has produced breeds with quite different personalities. The Westie (along with the Scottish Terrier) is recognized worldwide because of the part it plays in advertising a Scotch whisky. White is also a fashionable colour for dogs, signifying good luck, or simply cleanliness. The consequence is that the Westie is very popular in North America, Great Britain, Europe, and Japan. The breed has a very high incidence of allergic skin conditions, and an excitable temperament. It thrives on plenty of attention and regular exercise.

Hard-haired topcoat

KEY FACTS

COUNTRY OF ORIGIN Great Britain

DATE OF ORIGIN 1800s

FIRST USE Ratting

USE TODAY Companion

LIFE EXPECTANCY 14 years

WEIGHT RANGE
7–10 kg (15–22 lb)

HEIGHT RANGE
25–28 cm (10–11 in)

Small, erect ears have sharp tips

Slightly sunken eyes are set wide apart

Head is very thickly coated with hair

BREED HISTORY
The Cairn Terrier occasionally used to produce white puppies. The Malcolm family, of Scotland, selectively bred these, producing a breed easily visible on the Scottish moors.

SKYE TERRIER

Popular for centuries, the Skye Terrier was at one time the favoured dog of the royal courts of Scotland and England. Scotland's most famous dog, Greyfriar's Bobby, is said to have been a Skye Terrier. For 14 years after his master's death in the mid-1800s, despite being given good homes, Bobby escaped and revisited his master's favourite cafe each day until his own death. A statue in the dog's memory stands near Greyfriar's Church in Edinburgh, Scotland. Inclined to be snappy when provoked, and perhaps not ideal for children, the Skye can be intensely loyal.

BREED HISTORY This exceptionally long-haired terrier is named after its Scottish Hebridean island of origin. At one time it was used extensively for otter, badger, and weasel tracking. Now a popular companion, it is ideal for the city.

KEY FACTS

COUNTRY OF ORIGIN Great Britain

DATE OF ORIGIN 1600s

FIRST USE Small-game hunting

USE TODAY Companion

LIFE EXPECTANCY 13 years

WEIGHT RANGE
8.5–10.5 kg (19–23 lb)

HEIGHT RANGE
23–25 cm (9–10 in)

Abundant topcoat is long and straight

CREAM

FAWN

GREY

BLACK

Eyes are covered with hair

Nose is black, with large, wide nostrils

SCOTTISH TERRIER

This solid, quiet, and even dour dog has always been more popular in North America than in Great Britain. The American president Franklin Delano Roosevelt often travelled with his Scottie, Fala, and Walt Disney perpetuated the gentlemanly image of this breed in his film, *Lady and the Tramp*. Primarily a companion, the Scottie is reserved and a little aloof, and makes an excellent guardian.

KEY FACTS

COUNTRY OF ORIGIN Great Britain

DATE OF ORIGIN 1800s

FIRST USE Small-mammal hunting

USE TODAY Companion

LIFE EXPECTANCY 13–14 years

OTHER NAME Aberdeen Terrier

WEIGHT RANGE
8.5–10.5 kg (19–23 lb)

HEIGHT RANGE
25–28 cm (10–11 in)

Eyebrows are long and distinctive

Harsh, thick topcoat, with soft undercoat

BREED HISTORY The Scottie of today is probably a descendant of dogs from the Scottish Western Isles, which were selectively bred in Aberdeen in the mid-1800s.

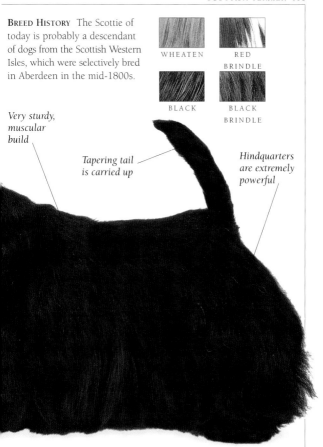

WHEATEN

RED BRINDLE

BLACK

BLACK BRINDLE

Very sturdy, muscular build

Tapering tail is carried up

Hindquarters are extremely powerful

DANDIE DINMONT TERRIER

Despite the variety of hypotheses as to whether the Dandie Dinmont originates from the Skye, Bedlington, or old-type Scottish Terriers, or the Otterhound or a basset breed from Flanders, one fact is indisputable. It does not have the typical "take-no-prisoners-alive" terrier mentality. This is a docile breed, although its bark is deep and massive, and when aroused, it is willing to fight. Neither quarrelsome nor snappy, it is an easygoing house dog, thriving on the companionship of both adults and children. It is also very loyal, and is a good guard dog. Although it enjoys vigorous exercise, it is quite content playing in the house or back garden. Sadly, its long back and short legs predispose it to rather painful invertebral problems.

KEY FACTS

COUNTRY OF ORIGIN Great Britain

DATE OF ORIGIN 1600s

FIRST USE Badger/rat hunting

USE TODAY Companion

LIFE EXPECTANCY 13–14 years

WEIGHT RANGE
8–11 kg (18–24 lb)

HEIGHT RANGE
20–28 cm (8–11 in)

PEPPER

MUSTARD

Wiry hair on top of tail

BREED HISTORY Curiously named after a country gentleman in Sir Walter Scott's novel, *Guy Mannering*, paintings show that the Dandie Dinmont was owned by aristocracy for centuries before it was named. It may have its ancient origins in the gypsies' dogs of southern Scotland.

Neck is strong and muscular

BEDLINGTON TERRIER

Legend says that the Whippet, Otterhound, and Dandie Dinmont are the forebears of this very distinctive breed. Certainly, the Bedlington's desire to "search and destroy" has been concealed under sheep's clothing – this unusual dog may look like a sheep, but it retains the terrier's need for mental stimulation, and can be destructive if it is denied sufficient physical activity.

Coat is blend of equal parts topcoat and undercoat

Muscular hind legs are like a Whippet's

KEY FACTS

COUNTRY OF ORIGIN Great Britain

DATE OF ORIGIN 1800s

FIRST USE Rat/badger hunting

USE TODAY Companion

LIFE EXPECTANCY 14–15 years

OTHER NAME Rothbury Terrier

WEIGHT RANGE
8–10 kg (17–23 lb)

HEIGHT RANGE
38–43 cm (15–17 in)

LIVER

SANDY

BLUE

Close-fitting lips

Fringe of white, silky hair has been left unclipped at ear tips

BREED HISTORY

Gypsies living in the Rothbury forest near the Scottish Borders once kept functional, speedy, working terriers, known as the Rothbury Terriers. It is likely that the Bedlington Terrier, first shown in 1870, in Bedlington, Northumberland, England, descends from these dogs.

SEALYHAM TERRIER

No longer used for its original purpose, the Sealyham is an attractive, bossy, and independent companion; it also makes a distinctive show dog. Its origins as a dog willing to take on badgers or otters on their own ground are evident in its frequently aggressive attitude to other dogs. Even after almost a century of breeding for companionship, males, in particular, still need firm and experienced handling. In the 1930s, the Sealyham was an extremely popular dog, especially in North America. Today, it is almost unknown outside English-speaking countries and is uncommon even in its land of origin.

BREED HISTORY The Sealyham was selectively bred by using a variety of terriers. This produced a superb badger and otter hunter, which was willing to work in burrows, above ground, and in water.

Remarkably powerful thighs

Long, wiry coat requires expert preparation for show ring

KEY FACTS

COUNTRY OF ORIGIN Great Britain

DATE OF ORIGIN 1870s

FIRST USE Badger/otter hunting

USE TODAY Companion

LIFE EXPECTANCY 14 years

WEIGHT RANGE
8–9 kg (18–20 lb)

HEIGHT RANGE
25–30 cm (10–12 in)

Dark, round, medium-sized eyes

Hair brushed forwards over eyes for show purposes

Ears have round tips

Long hair on face gives square appearance

Round, cat-like feet have thick pads

SMOOTH FOX TERRIER

E ach English county once had its own fox terrier. The genes of the extinct white Cheshire and Shropshire Terrier are probably still present in this breed, together with those of the Beagle. The Smooth Fox Terrier was once a classic working dog, but today it is foremost an attractive, although often obstinate and strong-willed, companion. With persistence, this athletic dog can be obedience trained. Its agility and joy in exercising off the lead make it a good breed for the countryside.

KEY FACTS

COUNTRY OF ORIGIN Great Britain

DATE OF ORIGIN 1700s

FIRST USE Fox flushing, vermin killing

USE TODAY Companion

LIFE EXPECTANCY 13–14 years

WEIGHT RANGE
7–8 kg (16–18 lb)

HEIGHT RANGE
38.5–39.5 cm (15 in)

WHITE

WHITE/
TAN

BLACK/
TAN

*Feet are round
and compact*

BREED HISTORY At one time, all dogs that went to earth chasing foxes were called fox terriers. It was not until 1850, however, that controlled breeding began, resulting in the breed of today.

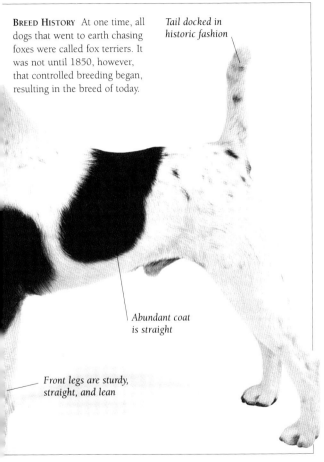

Tail docked in historic fashion

Abundant coat is straight

Front legs are sturdy, straight, and lean

WIRE FOX TERRIER

More popular than its Smooth relative, the Wire Fox Terrier did not appear in show rings until the 1870s, 20 years after its cousin. It has been an intermittently popular breed, fashionable in the 1930s, then out of favour until recently, when it re-emerged as a "classic" English breed. The Wire Fox is not demonstrative with people; it is wilful, and can be a bit snappy. One of the breed's instinctive traits that has not diminished over the years is its joy in digging. Its enjoyment in challenging other dogs to fights is almost as great. Deafness can be a problem in predominantly white individuals.

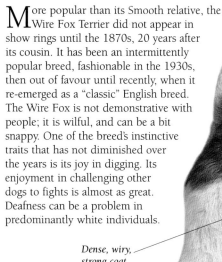

Dense, wiry, strong coat

Weight is evenly distributed

WHITE

WHITE/ BLACK

WHITE/ TAN

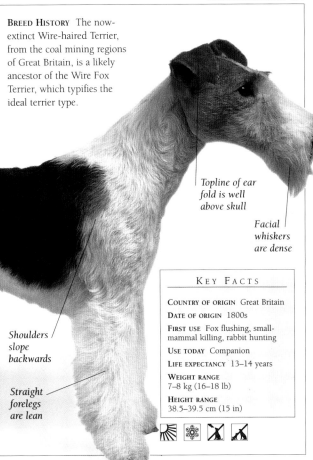

BREED HISTORY The now-extinct Wire-haired Terrier, from the coal mining regions of Great Britain, is a likely ancestor of the Wire Fox Terrier, which typifies the ideal terrier type.

Topline of ear fold is well above skull

Facial whiskers are dense

Shoulders slope backwards

Straight forelegs are lean

KEY FACTS

COUNTRY OF ORIGIN Great Britain

DATE OF ORIGIN 1800s

FIRST USE Fox flushing, small-mammal killing, rabbit hunting

USE TODAY Companion

LIFE EXPECTANCY 13–14 years

WEIGHT RANGE
7–8 kg (16–18 lb)

HEIGHT RANGE
38.5–39.5 cm (15 in)

PARSON JACK RUSSELL TERRIER

This is the less common version of Great Britain's most popular country terrier, the Jack Russell. The Parson Jack Russell conforms to its first breeder's requirement for long legs, which allowed the dog to keep up with horses on the hunt. The vicar who developed the breed preferred wire-haired dogs; today, smooth and wire coats are both permissible and are equally popular. Sprightly and robust, this breed is a good companion, but it does require regular exercise.

Amputated tail on working dogs only

Compact feet, with hair between toes

KEY FACTS

COUNTRY OF ORIGIN Great Britain

DATE OF ORIGIN 1800s

FIRST USE Hunting, fox bolting

USE TODAY Companion

LIFE EXPECTANCY 13–14 years

WEIGHT RANGE
5–8 kg (12–18 lb)

HEIGHT RANGE
28–38 cm (11–15 in)

WHITE/
BROWN

WHITE/
BLACK

TRICOLOUR

*High-set ears are
like dropped Vs*

*Wiry coat may be
broken or smooth, and
has good undercoat*

*Moustache and
beard give mature
appearance to face*

*Chest is not
too broad,
so dog can
enter fox hole*

*Nails are white
and only
moderately thick*

BREED HISTORY Reverend
Jack Russell, a sporting
parson from Devon, in
southwest England, and
a founding member of the
Kennel Club of Great
Britain, developed this
strain of wire-haired fox
terrier, which was long
enough in the leg to
accompany horses on the
hunt, and small enough
to burrow and bolt foxes.

JACK RUSSELL TERRIER

The feisty, exuberant, crowd-pleasing Jack Russell is a hyperactive bundle of muscles. This popular town or country dog can be snappy and aggressive with anything that moves (including people), but is fun loving and, in most instances, overwhelmingly affectionate both with its family and with strangers.

Long, rather pointed muzzle, with jet-black nose and black-pigmented lips

Relatively narrow chest

KEY FACTS

COUNTRY OF ORIGIN Great Britain

DATE OF ORIGIN 1800s

FIRST USE Ratting

USE TODAY Companion, ratting

LIFE EXPECTANCY 13–14 years

WEIGHT RANGE
4–7 kg (9–15 lb)

HEIGHT RANGE
25–26 cm (10–12 in)

BREED HISTORY Almost identical to the Parson Jack Russell but for its shorter legs and its more varied appearance, this breed is extremely popular in Great Britain. Originally bred to hunt and kill rats, it has retained its killer's instincts.

WHITE/ BROWN

WHITE/ BLACK

TRICOLOUR

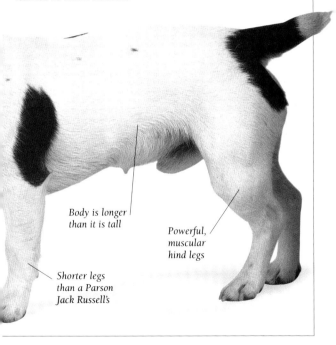

Body is longer than it is tall

Powerful, muscular hind legs

Shorter legs than a Parson Jack Russell's

MANCHESTER TERRIER

This sleek, athletic breed reached its height of popularity about 100 years ago, when it was known as the "English Gentleman's Terrier". Exported to North America and Germany, it has been erroneously credited with lending its black-and-tan coat colour to the development of the Dobermann. Its decline began when rat baiting became unfashionable. The ban on ear cropping further reduced its popularity, and it took some time for breeders to create its V-shaped, hanging ears. Although the Manchester Terrier is short tempered, it makes a fine, lively, and robust companion.

Thick, smooth, glossy, dense coat is not soft to the touch

KEY FACTS

COUNTRY OF ORIGIN Great Britain

DATE OF ORIGIN 1500s

FIRST USE Ratting, rabbit hunting

USE TODAY Companion

LIFE EXPECTANCY 13–14 years

OTHER NAME Black-and-tan Terrier

WEIGHT RANGE
5–10 kg (11–22 lb)

HEIGHT RANGE
38–41 cm (15–16 in)

Small, V-shaped ears are folded

Small, dark, sparkling eyes

Short body, with well-sprung ribs and slightly curved back

Wedge-shaped muzzle does not show any cheek muscles

BREED HISTORY
Vermin-hunting black-and-tan terriers existed in Great Britain for hundreds of years. John Hulme, a breeder from Manchester, England, is credited with crossing these terriers with the Whippet in the 1800s, producing this lithe, agile, and powerful ratter and rabbiter. Popular for a time, the Manchester is now rare.

Well-proportioned, straight, long forelimbs, with small feet

ENGLISH TOY TERRIER

A relatively rare terrier, even in its country of origin, the English Toy descends from runt Manchester Terriers. Italian Greyhound blood might have been introduced to stabilize its size, which could account for its slightly arched, or "roached", back, but its personality remains one hundred per cent terrier. Breeding has passed through various phases, emphasizing its tiny size, or arched back, or "candle-flame" ears. Breeding now appears stable, but on an international level it is unlikely that this effervescent little terrier will become as recognized or as popular as the similar Miniature Pinscher. It is, however, an enjoyable companion, and is ideally suited to the city.

Tail is thick at root and tapers to tip

Loins are well rounded

Feet are dainty and compact

BREED HISTORY This breed caused a sensation when it appeared about 100 years ago, but for some time it suffered from health-related problems. Breeders have focused on improving its constitution and its appearance.

Dramatic "candle-flame" ears are slightly pointed at tips

Wedge-shaped head is long and narrow, with flat skull

Chest is narrow and deep, with straight, thin front legs

Thick, smooth coat, with dense, short, glossy hair

KEY FACTS

COUNTRY OF ORIGIN Great Britain

DATE OF ORIGIN 1800s

FIRST USE Ratting, rabbit hunting

USE TODAY Companion

LIFE EXPECTANCY 12–13 years

OTHER NAMES Black-and-tan Toy Terrier, Toy Manchester Terrier

WEIGHT RANGE
3–4 kg (6–8 lb)

HEIGHT RANGE
25–30 cm (10–12 in)

BULL TERRIER

In the Bull Terrier, the Bulldog's strength was combined with the terrier's tenacity to create the ultimate fighting dog. The original breeder, James Hinks, favoured white Bull Terriers; unwittingly, in selecting for this colour he also selected for inherited deafness, chronic skin inflammations, and heart disease. Darker Bull Terriers have a much lower incidence of these conditions, although inherited juvenile kidney failure can occur. The breed does, however, have a lower-than-average tendency to snap and bite, and is good with people. When it does bite, the damage is considerable, since it does not let go easily.

KEY FACTS

COUNTRY OF ORIGIN Great Britain

DATE OF ORIGIN 1800s

FIRST USE Dog fighting, companion

USE TODAY Companion

LIFE EXPECTANCY 11–13 years

OTHER NAME English Bull Terrier

WEIGHT RANGE
24–28 kg (52–62 lb)

HEIGHT RANGE
53–56 cm (21–22 in)

Head curves downwards from tip of skull to tip of nose

Chest is extremely broad, with well-sprung ribs

Round, compact feet have neat toes

WHITE

FAWN

RED

TRICOLOUR

BLACK BRINDLE

Thin ears are set close together

BREED HISTORY The Bull Terrier was developed by James Hinks of Birmingham, England, who bred the Bulldog with the now-extinct White English Terrier to produce a dog that dazzled observers in both the dog-fighting pit and the show ring. Hinks' favoured white Bull Terriers also became, and remain, fashionable companions.

Short tail is carried horizontally

Shoulder blades are flat and wide

Well-muscled thighs

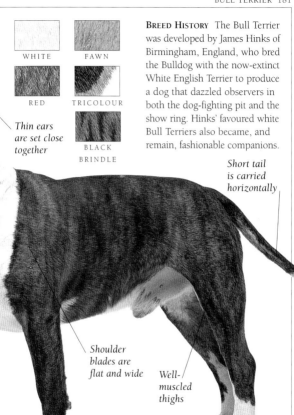

STAFFORDSHIRE BULL TERRIER

Here is a true split-personality dog, a genuine canine Jekyll-and-Hyde character. There is probably no breed that is more loving with its family, and often with strangers, even veterinarians, than this kinetic mass of solid bone and thick muscle. It thrives on affection and devotes itself to being accepted as part of its human family. However, when it sees another dog – or any other animal – it can quite suddenly reveal a different side of its character, as it becomes overwhelmed by a desire to destroy. Selective breeding has successfully reduced, but not eliminated, this tendency. The breed is internationally popular, and its numbers are likely to continue to increase worldwide.

BREED HISTORY Originating in Staffordshire, England, this well-muscled and exceedingly affectionate breed traces its ancestry to crosses between ferocious, thickly muscled bull baiters and agile, lithe, feisty local terriers. It was bred as a dual-purpose "sporting" dog, to participate in organized ratting and dog fighting.

Hind legs are well muscled yet perfectly parallel

Smooth, short, close-fitting coat is almost any colour except black and tan, or liver

Short, deep head, with very broad skull

Small, wide-set, half-prick ears fall away from cheeks

Round, medium-sized eyes set to look straight ahead, giving good binocular vision

Cheek muscles are very pronounced and powerful

Forelegs are set wide apart

Medium-sized, strong, well-padded feet

KEY FACTS

COUNTRY OF ORIGIN Great Britain

DATE OF ORIGIN 1800s

FIRST USE Dog fighting, ratting

USE TODAY Companion

LIFE EXPECTANCY 11–12 years

WEIGHT RANGE
11–17 kg (24–38 lb)

HEIGHT RANGE
36–41 cm (14–16 in)

VARIETY

OF

COLOURS

AMERICAN STAFFORDSHIRE TERRIER

Like its close British relative, the American Staffordshire Terrier can be extremely gentle and affectionate with children and adults, and at the same time potentially lethal with other dogs. All members of the breed, but males in particular, need early socialization with other animals to ensure that they do not follow their instinct to attack. Most commonly seen with uncropped ears, the breed is almost always a loyal and obedient canine member of the family. It does, however, descend from bull biters and pit fighters, and still has the jaw power and tenacity to inflict horrific wounds.

BREED HISTORY Originally identical to the British Staffordshire Bull Terrier, the American was selectively bred for greater height and weight, and a bulkier build. In 1936, it was recognized as a separate breed.

ANY COLOUR

Short, heavily muscled neck blends into strong forelimbs

KEY FACTS

COUNTRY OF ORIGIN United States

DATE OF ORIGIN 1800s

FIRST USE Bull baiting/fighting

USE TODAY Companion

LIFE EXPECTANCY 12 years

WEIGHT RANGE
18–23 kg (40–50 lb)

HEIGHT RANGE
43–48 cm (17–19 in)

Medium-length, tapered tail

Front legs are very long and thickly boned

Feet are strong, with thickly cushioned pads

BOSTON TERRIER

Well mannered, thoughtful, and considerate, this true
New Englander is a perennially popular dog in North
America, making a sprightly, entertaining, active, and
durable companion. Terrier in name only, it has lost any
ruthless desire for mayhem, preferring the company of
humans, although male Bostons will still challenge other
dogs if they feel their territory has been invaded.
As with other proportionally large-headed
breeds, Caesarean operations are sometimes
needed to deliver puppies. Breeders have,
however, been successful in reducing the
size of the head, while retaining the dog's
unique and quirky good looks.

*Thighs are
strong and
well
muscled*

KEY FACTS

COUNTRY OF ORIGIN United States

DATE OF ORIGIN 1800s

FIRST USE Ratting, companion

USE TODAY Companion

LIFE EXPECTANCY 13 years

OTHER NAME Boston Bull

WEIGHT RANGE
4.5–11.5 kg (10–25 lb)

HEIGHT RANGE
38–43 cm (15–17 in)

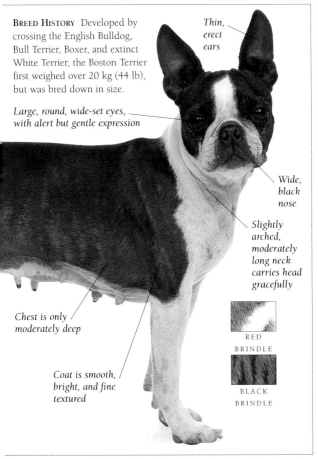

BREED HISTORY Developed by crossing the English Bulldog, Bull Terrier, Boxer, and extinct White Terrier, the Boston Terrier first weighed over 20 kg (44 lb), but was bred down in size.

Thin, erect ears

Large, round, wide-set eyes, with alert but gentle expression

Wide, black nose

Slightly arched, moderately long neck carries head gracefully

Chest is only moderately deep

Coat is smooth, bright, and fine textured

RED BRINDLE

BLACK BRINDLE

AMERICAN TOY TERRIER

This robust little terrier retains all the passion of its fox terrier ancestors. It is tough and bright, but stubborn, and equally at home on a farm or in a city. The American Toy makes an excellent ratter, but more often it serves as an extension to the family, entertaining all with its energetic and youthful antics. It has also proved to be an excellent hearing dog for deaf people – it can be trained to take its human companion to the sources of sounds such as the telephone.

KEY FACTS

COUNTRY OF ORIGIN United States

DATE OF ORIGIN 1930s

FIRST USE Ratting

USE TODAY Companion

LIFE EXPECTANCY 13–14 years

OTHER NAME Toy Fox Terrier, Amertoy

WEIGHT RANGE
2–3 kg (4½–7 lb)

HEIGHT RANGE
24.5–25.5 cm (10 in)

WHITE/ TAN

TRICOLOUR

BLACK/ WHITE

Straight, thin forelegs

BREED HISTORY This breed, which was recognized in 1936, was developed by crossing "runts" from Smooth Fox Terrier litters with the English Toy Terrier and Chihuahua.

Ears are large, V-shaped, and stand erect

Small, narrow muzzle; skull not as dramatically domed as a Chihuahua's

Tail is docked due to demands of fashion

Coat is smooth, with short, straight hair

Feet are dainty and compact

MINIATURE PINSCHER

Strikingly similar in appearance to the English Toy Terrier, the Miniature Pinscher evolved along completely different lines, but for the same purpose – that of rodent control. Although it looks like a tiny Dobermann, it is related to that breed only by country of origin, and predates it by perhaps 200 years. Today, this feisty little terrier (*pinscher* is German for terrier or biter) is kept strictly as a companion, but its ratting ability remains fully developed. In spite of its size, it will quite happily challenge dogs that are 10 times larger than itself, and has a tendency to snap first and ask questions later.

Tail has been amputated – an illegal mutilation in many countries

When standing naturally, hind legs are well separated

KEY FACTS

COUNTRY OF ORIGIN Germany

DATE OF ORIGIN 1700s

FIRST USE Ratting

USE TODAY Companion

LIFE EXPECTANCY 13–14 years

OTHER NAME Zwergpinscher

WEIGHT RANGE
4–5 kg (8–10 lb)

HEIGHT RANGE
25–30 cm (10–12 in)

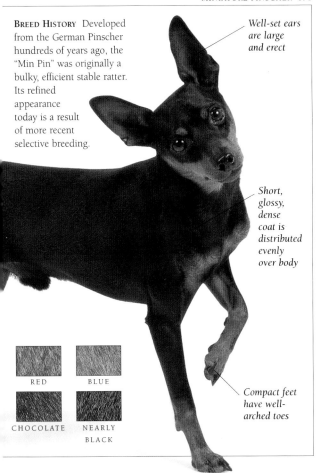

BREED HISTORY Developed from the German Pinscher hundreds of years ago, the "Min Pin" was originally a bulky, efficient stable ratter. Its refined appearance today is a result of more recent selective breeding.

Well-set ears are large and erect

Short, glossy, dense coat is distributed evenly over body

Compact feet have well-arched toes

RED

BLUE

CHOCOLATE

NEARLY BLACK

GERMAN PINSCHER

With its sleek, handsome looks and medium-sized build, the German Pinscher should be an ideal companion dog, but inexplicably, it is now a rare breed. It is lively but docile, quite versatile, and in addition to being a good and vocal guard dog, responds reasonably well to obedience training. Like other pinschers and terriers, it does not back away from disputes with other dogs, and needs firm handling to control its pugilistic tendencies.

FAWN

DARK BROWN

BLACK/ TAN

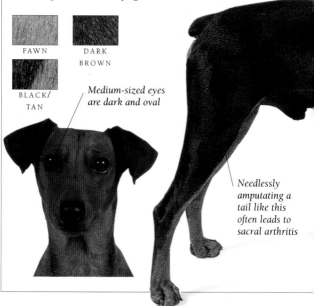

Medium-sized eyes are dark and oval

Needlessly amputating a tail like this often leads to sacral arthritis

BREED HISTORY This tall terrier evolved as a traditional farmer's multi-purpose dog. It controlled vermin, guarded and drove livestock, and served as a watchdog. It is the forebear of the Miniature Pinscher, and played a role in the development of the Dobermann.

Ears have been cropped; uncut ears are high set with natural half fold

Long muzzle is bluntly tipped with black nose

Short coat is strong, smooth, and glossy

Body is robust and well muscled, like a schnauzer's

KEY FACTS

COUNTRY OF ORIGIN Germany

DATE OF ORIGIN 1700s

FIRST USE Vermin hunting

USE TODAY Companion

LIFE EXPECTANCY 12–14 years

OTHER NAME Standard Pinscher

WEIGHT RANGE
11–16 kg (25–35 lb)

HEIGHT RANGE
41–48 cm (16–19 in)

AFFENPINSCHER

The seriousness, intensity, and humour of this sparky breed can bring a smile to the face of the most preoccupied person. It looks like a cartoon but in fact, even with its compressed jaws, the Affenpinscher still makes a formidable ratter when given the opportunity. It is also an efficient quail and rabbit tracker. Stubborn and opinionated, it does not respond well to obedience training, and has a tendency to snap. It does, however, make a lively and amusing companion. Today, the breed is rare in Germany, the largest numbers surviving in North America. A larger variety of the Affenpinscher became extinct at the beginning of the 1900s.

KEY FACTS

COUNTRY OF ORIGIN Germany

DATE OF ORIGIN 1600s

FIRST USE Vermin hunting

USE TODAY Companion

LIFE EXPECTANCY 14–15 years

OTHER NAME Monkey Dog

WEIGHT RANGE
3–3.5 kg (7–8 lb)

HEIGHT RANGE
25–30 cm (10–12 in)

Tail has short hair and is carried high when dog is standing

Large, dark eyes have bushy brows

Face is covered in coarse hair

Abundant moustache and beard

Broad chest is covered with dense, dry hair

BREED HISTORY This ancient breed's precise history is unknown. Its anatomy suggests that it was developed from crossing small, local pinschers with pug-like dogs from Asia. It is probably the parent of the Belgian griffons, and a relative of the Miniature Schnauzer.

MINIATURE SCHNAUZER

Named after its most prominent physical feature (in German, *schnauze* means nose or snout), the Miniature Schnauzer is less noisy and feisty than British terriers, and has become one of North America's favourite town companions. The breed is calm, easy to obedience train, and is not snappy. Good with children and other dogs, it is happy to settle into the routines of its human family. An enthusiastic barker, it is also an excellent guard dog. It sheds little hair, but its coat needs constant attention. Sadly, increased popularity has encouraged indiscriminate breeding, and inherited medical problems are now relatively common. So, too, is a rather nervous disposition.

Good angles to hind legs allow for powerful bursts of speed

KEY FACTS

COUNTRY OF ORIGIN Germany

DATE OF ORIGIN 1400s

FIRST USE Ratting

USE TODAY Companion

LIFE EXPECTANCY 14 years

OTHER NAME Zwergschnauzer

WEIGHT RANGE
6–7 kg (13–15 lb)

HEIGHT RANGE
30–36 cm (12–14 in)

BREED HISTORY Almost a perfect replica of the Giant and Standard Schnauzers, the Miniature descends from this root stock, with the addition of Affenpinscher and Miniature Pinscher bloodlines. It is unlikely, as some sources suggest, that poodles played a role in the development of the breed.

Eyes are naturally shaded with bushy, bristly eyebrows

Small ears are high set, and almost fully dropped

Topcoat is quite hard and coarse; undercoat is soft

Under well-trimmed fur, feet are much like those of a cat

BLACK/
SILVER

PEPPER/
SALT

BLACK

DACHSHUNDS

The international name of dachshund, meaning badger dog, reflects these breeds' original purpose. For the last 100 years they have been bred as "earth dogs", the standard size being willing and able to follow badgers and foxes to earth, with the miniature version doing the same with rabbits. Show-standard dogs have deep chests and short legs, while working dogs have less robust chests and longer legs. In Germany, where these resilient dogs are still worked, they are categorized by chest circumference. The Kaninchenteckel (Rabbit-hunting Dachshund) has a maximum 30 cm (12 in) chest measurement, the Zwergteckel (Miniature) measures from 31–35 cm (12–14 in), and the Normalschlag (Standard) measures over 35 cm (14 in). All dachshunds are of hound origin, but because of their utilitarian role as Germany's most effective earth dogs, these breeds are aptly classified with the other earth dogs – the terrier group. Today, most dachshunds are kept as household companions, and they are perhaps the most recognizable of all breeds.

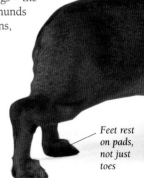

BREED HISTORY Ancient Egyptian sculptures show a pharaoh seated with three short-legged dogs. The dachshund's ancestors may date back to these dwarf dogs. The Smooth-haired Standard is perhaps the oldest dachshund.

Feet rest on pads, not just toes

KEY FACTS

COUNTRY OF ORIGIN Germany

DATE OF ORIGIN 1900s

FIRST USE Badger flushing

USE TODAY Companion

LIFE EXPECTANCY 14–17 years

OTHER NAMES Zwergteckel
(Miniature), Normalschlag
(Standard)

WEIGHT RANGE Miniature: 4–5 kg
(9–10 lb); Standard: 6.5–11.5 kg
(15–25 lb)

HEIGHT RANGE Miniature and
Standard 13–25 cm (5–10 in)

*Short, dense,
lustrous coat*

*Neck is
carried
with
dignity*

VARIETY
OF
COLOURS

SMOOTH-HAIRED
STANDARD DACHSHUND

BREED HISTORY The Wire-haired was created by crossing the Smooth-haired with rough-haired pinschers. This produced a dog with a rough coat but a small head; further crosses with the short-legged Dandie Dinmont Terrier enlarged and elongated the head, while at the same time injecting a degree of control to the dachshund's innate bloodlust.

WIRE-HAIRED MINIATURE DACHSHUND

Distinctive bushy eyebrows and beard

Nose not as tapered as that of Smooth-haired

Topcoat is thick and wiry, yet lies flat

Feet have closely set toes

BREED HISTORY The Long-haired Standard Dachshund was probably developed by crossing the Smooth-haired Standard Dachshund with short-legged spaniels, similar to the Sussex or Field Spaniel, and then miniaturizing the result. The Long-haired certainly has an affectionate, outgoing personality similar to that of spaniels.

LONG-HAIRED STANDARD DACHSHUND

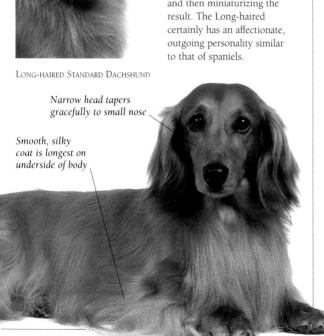

Narrow head tapers gracefully to small nose

Smooth, silky coat is longest on underside of body

CZESKY TERRIER

The Czesky Terrier's unique looks have made it a favourite companion in its home countries, the Czech and Slovak republics. In the 1980s, however, Czech and Slovak breeders felt that it had deteriorated from its original form and function, and it was again crossed with the Sealyham Terrier. The Czesky has all the ground terrier's typical attributes – it is a feisty, persistent, stubborn, and fearless dog, strong enough to subdue animals much larger than itself. Its coat requires constant attention and, like most terriers, it has a tendency to snap. Apart from this, it is an alert, inquisitive, and affable breed.

BLUE-
GREY

TAWNY

*Robust tail is
carried down
when relaxed*

*Dark, wavy hair
on legs is not
usually clipped*

KEY FACTS

COUNTRY OF ORIGIN Czech Republic

DATE OF ORIGIN 1940s

FIRST USE Burrowing

USE TODAY Companion, hunting

LIFE EXPECTANCY 12–14 years

OTHER NAMES Czech Terrier, Bohemian Terrier

WEIGHT RANGE
5.5–8 kg (12–18 lb)

HEIGHT RANGE
28–36 cm (10–14 in)

BREED HISTORY Geneticist Dr. Frantisek Horak crossed the Sealyham and Scottish, and perhaps the Dandie Dinmont Terriers to create a breed that worked like a German hunting terrier, but with shorter legs more suited to working underground.

Hair is not clipped on head, leaving prominent beard and eyebrows

GRIFFON BRUXELLOIS

The Griffon Bruxellois is a classic "Euro-dog" – the result of blending bloodlines from diverse regions to produce a good-natured, amusing, alert, and reliable companion. There is confusion about its name – in some countries three similar dogs are classified as the Belgian Griffon. In other countries each of these dogs is recognized as unique, and is given its own name. The breed reached its greatest numbers in the period between the World Wars. Today, it has been superseded in popularity by one of its ancestors, the Yorkshire Terrier, and remains most popular in Belgium.

KEY FACTS

COUNTRY OF ORIGIN Belgium
DATE OF ORIGIN 1800s
FIRST USE Vermin hunting
USE TODAY Companion
LIFE EXPECTANCY 12–14 years
OTHER NAME Griffon Belge
WEIGHT RANGE
2.5–5.5 kg (6–12 lb)
HEIGHT RANGE
18–20 cm (7–8 in)

Small, black nose set deeply back between eyes

BLACK/
TAN

BLACK

Profuse, wiry, red beard gives sagacious look to face

Forelegs are well muscled and boned

BREED HISTORY The Dutch Smoushond, German Affenpinscher, French Barbet (a possible forerunner of the poodle), and Yorkshire Terrier have probably been used to produce today's Brussels Griffon.

GUNDOGS

FOR THOUSANDS OF YEARS, hunters in search of food or in pursuit of sport were accompanied by sight and scent hounds. With the introduction of firearms to hunting, breeders focused on traits such as coat texture, length of bone, scenting ability, and levels of obedience, to produce highly responsive and effective workers. Today, these trustworthy breeds are some of the world's most popular canine companions.

Weimaraner

BREEDING FOR ABILITY

Hunting by sight or scent, going to earth, guarding, and swimming are all natural dog behaviours that require little additional training. However, finding game, then standing or crouching absolutely still, or leaping forth on command into cold water to pick up a shot bird and then carry it in the mouth back to the hunter, demands both instinctive ability and a willingness to be trained. In the l700s and 1800s, from a genetic base of hounds and herders, breeders produced over 50 breeds of gundog. Gundogs are usually divided into five subgroups – water dogs, pointers, setters, flushing dogs, and retrievers. Proficient water work requires a tight, waterproof coat and a strong desire to swim. The pointer searches for game silently, but rather than instinctively moving to capture its prey, it freezes perfectly still, often with one foreleg raised and bent, and "points". A setter behaves in the same way, except that it crouches down, or "sets".

EVOLVING POINTERS AND SETTERS

In the 1500s, Spanish pointers were exported to Great Britain and were probably crossed with sight and scent hounds to produce today's pointer. Spanish dogs were also involved in the development of British setters. In Germany, with the decline of field sports after the 1848 revolutions, local pointing and setting breeds virtually disappeared. Then around 1890, in an explosion of creative activity, breeders

Large Munsterlander

produced pointers in three coat types –
the Weimaraner, Munsterlander, and,
in the German-speaking parts of
Czechoslovakia, the Czesky Fousek.

BRITISH SPANIELS AND RETRIEVERS
British breeders produced flushing
spaniels, which flushed birds from
undergrowth. First dubbed land, field,
or water spaniels, for their favoured
terrain, they were later classified into
distinct breeds, including "cockers"
and "springers". Water dogs from
Newfoundland, Canada, were used to
create retrievers, dogs with an instinct
to carry prey gently in the mouth and
a great willingness to learn and obey.
Today, the Labrador and Golden
Retrievers are popular gundogs and
companions, and the most successful
assistance dogs for the disabled.

REGIONAL DEVELOPMENTS
While Denmark produced its own
pointer, the Netherlands some fine
small retrievers, and Hungary the

elegant Vizsla, French breeders
created a superb selection of gundogs.
Recently, there has been a renewed
interest in old gundog breeds, such
as the Italian Spinone, while Spanish
and Slovakian hunters continue to
develop their own unique gundogs.

ADMIRABLE ATTRIBUTES
Gundogs are generally easier to train
than any other group of dogs. They
are almost invariably relaxed with
children, are less inclined than other
dogs to fight among themselves, and,
in most cases, willingly
obey commands.

**German Short-
haired Pointer**

HUNGARIAN PULI

The responsive, obedient, and virtually waterproof Puli is almost certainly the ancestor of the poodle. Well into the 1900s, Hungarian shepherds continued to breed carefully for working ability. World War II virtually destroyed dog breeding in Hungary, but by then the Puli had been adopted as a companion. Hungarian immigrants established the Puli abroad, particularly in North America. This adaptable dog enjoys working sheep and can easily be trained to retrieve from water.

KEY FACTS

COUNTRY OF ORIGIN Hungary

DATE OF ORIGIN Middle Ages

FIRST USE Sheep herding

USE TODAY Companion, obedience, retrieving

LIFE EXPECTANCY 12–13 years

OTHER NAMES Hungarian Water Dog, Puli

WEIGHT RANGE
10–15 kg (22–33 lb)

HEIGHT RANGE
37–44 cm (14½–17½ in)

Ears are not noticeable

Slightly rusty colour is not uncommon

Some cords grow to floor length

WHITE

APRICOT

BLACK

BREED HISTORY The Puli (leader in Hungarian) was probably brought to Hungary by the Magyars. Today's Pulis come mainly from a breeding programme over the last century.

Fine, round head is hidden by hair

Each cord of hair has to be groomed separately

STANDARD POODLE

The Standard Poodle is not simply a fashion accessory – it is a responsive, easy-to-train, and reliable companion, guard, and retriever. The breed has a lower-than-average incidence of skin complaints and does not moult, making it an ideal dog for people who have allergies. Dependable, calm, and not given to the hysterics that sometimes afflict its smaller relatives, the Standard remains at heart a working dog. Its French name, Caniche, meaning duck dog, is descriptive of its original purpose – a duck retriever.

Hair left on tail gives buoyancy while swimming

KEY FACTS

COUNTRY OF ORIGIN Germany

DATE OF ORIGIN Middle Ages

FIRST USE Waterfowl retrieving

USE TODAY Companion, security

LIFE EXPECTANCY 11–15 years

OTHER NAMES Caniche, Barbone

WEIGHT RANGE
20.5–32 kg (45–70 lb)

HEIGHT RANGE
37.5–38.5 cm (15 in)

ALL
SOLID
COLOURS

*Head is well
proportioned
and dignified*

*Slightly
slanted,
alert-
looking
eyes*

*Solid, long,
straight muzzle
is not pointed*

*Hair on feet
increases
swimming
power*

BREED HISTORY
Drawings by artists such
as Albrecht Dürer reveal
that the poodle was
originally a water dog.
Today's clipping style
is based on historic
grooming to reduce
water resistance over the
powerful hindquarters
while working.

PORTUGUESE WATER DOG

This ancient breed of fisherman's dog has been used to pull nets in the water, as a message bearer swimming from boat to boat, and on land as a successful rabbiter. The breed is strong, loyal, and slightly suspicious by nature. Its coat was originally cut in a distinctive way in order to prevent its hind legs from dragging while swimming, and to protect its chest from thermal shock in cold water.

Domed head is large

WHITE

BROWN

BLACK

BLACK/ WHITE

BROWN/ WHITE

Long, wavy hair requires frequent grooming

BREED HISTORY This breed's ancestors arrived in Portugal either in the 400s with Visigoths from central Europe, or in the 700s with Moors from North Africa.

Plume of hair permits tail to float

KEY FACTS

COUNTRY OF ORIGIN Portugal

DATE OF ORIGIN Middle Ages

FIRST USE Working with fishermen

USE TODAY Companion, guarding, retrieving

LIFE EXPECTANCY 12–14 years

OTHER NAME Cão de Agua

WEIGHT RANGE
16–25 kg (35–55 lb)

HEIGHT RANGE
43–57 cm (17–22½ in)

Single coat can be either long or short

Hair clipped for work and showing

Chest is deep, with long, well-sprung ribs

Long legs from hocks down

SPANISH WATER DOG

This breed has not received much attention from professional breeders, one consequence being that both coat colour and body size vary considerably. Another is that inherited defects are less common in the Spanish Water Dog than in other dogs that have been more selectively bred. Although individuals can be found on the north coast of Spain, the majority live in the south, where they are now used primarily for goat herding, but also for retrieving ducks. The breed is not difficult to obedience train, and is not snappy, but can get irritable with children.

Heavy topknot covers eyes

WHITE

CHESTNUT

WHITE/
CHESTNUT

BLACK

KEY FACTS

COUNTRY OF ORIGIN Spain

DATE OF ORIGIN Middle Ages

FIRST USE Working with fishermen, goat herding, hunting

USE TODAY Companion, hunting

LIFE EXPECTANCY 10–14 years

OTHER NAME Perro de Aguas

WEIGHT RANGE
12–20 kg (26½–44 lb)

HEIGHT RANGE
38–50 cm (15–20 in)

Non-shedding coat forms heavy cords of hair

Hair bleaches in sunshine

Well-muscled hind legs provide endurance for swimming

BREED HISTORY
Related to the Portuguese Water Dog and perhaps to the poodle, this breed is still almost unknown outside Spain. It is a multi-purpose breed, assisting in herding, hunting, and fishing.

Paws have webbed toes

IRISH WATER SPANIEL

This breed, the most idiosyncratic of all spaniels, is the survivor of the three varieties of water spaniel that once inhabited Ireland. Its immense stamina, excellent swimming ability, virtually waterproof coat, and muscular power make it an ideal retriever, particularly for working the cold winter waters of the tidal estuaries of Ireland. Although this is a gentle, faithful, attentive companion, as well as an excellent gundog, it has never become a popular house dog. It is, however, ideal for country walkers.

Low-set, straight, tapering tail

Powerful thigh muscles

KEY FACTS

COUNTRY OF ORIGIN Ireland

DATE OF ORIGIN 1800s

FIRST USE Waterfowl retrieving

USE TODAY Companion, waterfowl retrieving

LIFE EXPECTANCY 12–14 years

OTHER NAMES Whip Tail, Bog Dog

WEIGHT RANGE
20–30 kg (45–65 lb)

HEIGHT RANGE
51–58 cm (20–23 in)

BREED HISTORY Portuguese fishermen might have introduced their Water Dog to Ireland while visiting Galway. Ancestors could, however, include the poodle.

Long, curly topknot of hair often hangs just above eyes

Very long, low-set ears close to cheeks, and covered with twisted curls

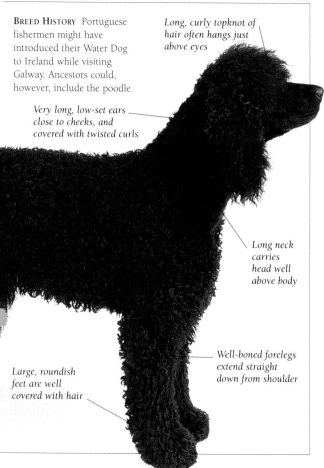

Long neck carries head well above body

Well-boned forelegs extend straight down from shoulder

Large, roundish feet are well covered with hair

CURLY-COATED RETRIEVER

A classic water dog, the Curly-coat remains the least common of all retrievers, although at one time it was used extensively in Great Britain to retrieve from water. It has a superb water dog's coat, composed of crisp, tight, small, waterproof curls. Hip dysplasia can occur in some Curly-coats; tight lower eyelids (entropion) also occur with greater-than-average frequency. However, this is a delightfully old-fashioned breed – calm and even tempered, but very alert when it is working.

Small ears are set at eye level and hang close to sides of head

Black nose sits at end of long, strong jaws

BREED HISTORY This is the oldest of the British retrievers, and evidence suggests that it existed as early as 1803. It probably descends from two now-extinct breeds, the English Water Spaniel and the Lesser Newfoundland, which was brought to Great Britain by cod fishermen.

KEY FACTS

COUNTRY OF ORIGIN Great Britain

DATE OF ORIGIN 1800s

FIRST USE Waterfowl retrieving

USE TODAY Gundog, companion

LIFE EXPECTANCY 12–13 years

WEIGHT RANGE
32–36 kg (70–80 lb)

HEIGHT RANGE
64–69 cm (25–27 in)

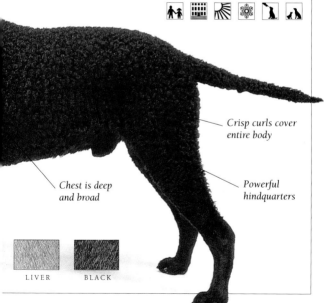

Crisp curls cover entire body

Chest is deep and broad

Powerful hindquarters

LIVER   BLACK

FLAT-COATED RETRIEVER

Bred in Great Britain from imported Newfoundland stock, the sleek Flat-coat was the favoured dog of British gamekeepers by the beginning of the 20th century. With the advent of the Labrador and Golden Retrievers, however, it was virtually extinct by the end of World War II. Today's handsome, humorous breed, fashionable once more as a gundog, is a superb flusher, and an excellent land and water retriever. Gregarious and versatile, its popularity is bound to increase, although it does suffer from a higher-than-average incidence of bone cancer.

Dark, medium-sized eyes have alert, questioning expression

KEY FACTS

COUNTRY OF ORIGIN Great Britain

DATE OF ORIGIN 1800s

FIRST USE Game retrieving

USE TODAY Companion, gundog, field trials

LIFE EXPECTANCY 12–14 years

WEIGHT RANGE
25–35 kg (60–80 lb)

HEIGHT RANGE
56–61 cm (22–24 in)

Short, flattened tail is moderately feathered with hair

BREED HISTORY Crossings
between the Newfoundland
and the now-extinct smaller
working dog from the St.
John's region of Newfoundland,
Canada, produced the Wavy-
coated Retriever. Further
crossings with setters resulted
in the effervescent Flat-coat.

LIVER   BLACK

*Dense, shiny, fine
coat lies flat, and
has waterproof
undercoat*

*Round,
strong feet,
with close,
well-arched
toes*

LABRADOR RETRIEVER

Waterproof, water-loving, affable, gregarious, and family oriented – a delicious range of adjectives describes one of the world's most popular family companions. The Labrador once worked from the shores of the granite-rocked inlets of the Newfoundland coast, retrieving the cork floats of fishing nets and swimming them ashore, so that fishermen could pull in the fish-filled nets. Today, this steadfast breed is the quintessence of the agreeable canine member of the human family. Unfortunately, many individuals do not live up to the image they carry. Some suffer from hereditary cataracts, hip and elbow arthritis, and even wayward temperaments. Despite this, the Labrador Retriever is one of the most loyal and dependable breeds in the world.

KEY FACTS

COUNTRY OF ORIGIN Great Britain

DATE OF ORIGIN 1800s

FIRST USE Gundog

USE TODAY Companion, gundog, field trials, assistance dog

LIFE EXPECTANCY 12–14 years

WEIGHT RANGE
25–34 kg (55–75 lb)

HEIGHT RANGE
54–57 cm (21½–22½ in)

Tail is very thick at base

Medium-length tail is covered in dense, short hair

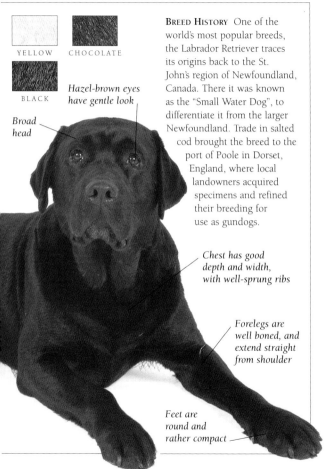

YELLOW   CHOCOLATE

BLACK

Hazel-brown eyes have gentle look

Broad head

BREED HISTORY One of the world's most popular breeds, the Labrador Retriever traces its origins back to the St. John's region of Newfoundland, Canada. There it was known as the "Small Water Dog", to differentiate it from the larger Newfoundland. Trade in salted cod brought the breed to the port of Poole in Dorset, England, where local landowners acquired specimens and refined their breeding for use as gundogs.

Chest has good depth and width, with well-sprung ribs

Forelegs are well boned, and extend straight from shoulder

Feet are round and rather compact

GOLDEN RETRIEVER

Relaxed but responsive, calm but alert, sensible and serene, the Golden is, in many ways, the ideal family companion. This affection-demanding, multi-purpose, easy-to-train, and attractive breed is even more popular in North America and Scandinavia than in its native Great Britain. Bred to retrieve waterfowl, it has a gentle mouth and will rarely snap or bite – it is especially patient with children. Different breed lines have evolved for different purposes. One variety works as a gundog, another has been developed for use in field trials, while the largest line is devoted to the show ring and family life. A fourth breeding line has produced dogs that are trained exclusively as assistants for blind or disabled people. Popularity has unfortunately produced inherited defects in some lines, such as allergic skin conditions, eye problems, and even irritable snappiness.

BREED HISTORY Records reveal that this gentle breed was developed in the late 1800s, by crossing a light-coloured Flat-coated Retriever with the now-extinct Tweed Water Spaniel. The first Goldens were exhibited in 1908.

Coat can be flat or wavy, with water-proof undercoat

Well-muscled hind legs are covered in thick skin and dense hair

KEY FACTS

COUNTRY OF ORIGIN Great Britain

DATE OF ORIGIN 1800s

FIRST USE Game retrieving

USE TODAY Companion, gundog, field trials, assistance dog

LIFE EXPECTANCY 13–15 years

WEIGHT RANGE
27–36 kg (60–80 lb)

HEIGHT RANGE
51–61cm (20–24 in)

CREAM

GOLD

Ears hang with slight fold

Eyes have kind expression

Dark, drooping lower lips

Forelimbs have long fringe of hair

Cat-like feet have copious hair between pads

Coat colour varies from cream to gold, and gets lighter with age

NOVA SCOTIA DUCK TOLLING RETRIEVER

The Toller's rather unusual job is to entice ducks and geese within shotgun range, and to retrieve them from the water after they have been hit. From his concealed blind near the shore, the hunter repeatedly tosses a stick parallel to the shore, which the Toller silently retrieves. When ducks or geese, attracted by the activity, come within shooting range, the hunter calls his dog back to the blind, stands up to put the birds to flight, and shoots. The Toller then acts as an efficient retriever.

KEY FACTS

COUNTRY OF ORIGIN Canada

DATE OF ORIGIN 1800s

FIRST USE Waterfowl flushing/retrieving

USE TODAY Gundog, companion

LIFE EXPECTANCY 12–14 years

OTHER NAMES Little River Duck Dog, Yarmouth Toller

WEIGHT RANGE
17–23 kg (37–51 lb)

HEIGHT RANGE
43–53 cm (17–21 in)

Head is clean cut and slightly wedge shaped

Deep chest is well insulated for cold-water swimming

Coat is dense, and occurs in various shades of red and orange

BREED HISTORY It is likely that tolling (from the Old English *tollen*, to entice) Red Decoy Dogs accompanied their masters from Great Britain to Nova Scotia, Canada. Crossed with retrievers and working spaniels, the breed was recognized in 1945.

Triangular ears are set high and well back on skull

Powerful, compact, well-muscled body on sturdy, solid legs

KOOIKERHONDJE

Historically, the Kooikerhondje behaved in much the same way as the now-extinct English Red Decoy Dog. With its lively antics and bushy white tail, it enticed ducks and geese towards nets, or within shotgun range. Kooikerhondjes are still used to entice ducks, but now they do so into traps made of rush matting, for banding and identification. Only 25 of these actively curious dogs survived World War II. These are the forebears of the approximately 500 new puppies registered each year. Due to this small genetic pool, inherited diseases do occur. However, this friendly, even-tempered breed makes a very satisfying companion.

Body is approximately as high as it is long

Heavy and luxurious topcoat conceals layer of insulating down

KEY FACTS

COUNTRY OF ORIGIN
The Netherlands

DATE OF ORIGIN 1700s

FIRST USE Bird flushing/retrieving

USE TODAY Companion, gundog

LIFE EXPECTANCY 12–13 years

OTHER NAMES Dutch Decoy Spaniel, Kooiker Dog

WEIGHT RANGE
9–11 kg (20–24 lb)

HEIGHT RANGE
35–41 cm (14–16 in)

BREED HISTORY Dating back at least to the time of William of Orange, this breed virtually disappeared, but was recreated between the World Wars by Baroness v. Hardenbroek van Ammerstool.

Ears have distinctive, wispy black hair

Moderately deep chest is covered with protective, waterproof hair

CHESAPEAKE BAY RETRIEVER

Although the Chesapeake Bay Retriever may trace its origins back to the small water dogs of Newfoundland, Canada, in form and function it is remarkably similar to the Curly-coated Retriever. This tireless worker excels at retrieving game and is a tougher breed than the Labrador Retriever, with a sharper personality. Like other retrievers, it is gentle with children and cordial to strangers. A loyal companion, it is happiest in a country setting.

KEY FACTS

COUNTRY OF ORIGIN United States

DATE OF ORIGIN 1900s

FIRST USE Waterfowl retrieving

USE TODAY Companion, gundog

LIFE EXPECTANCY 12–13 years

WEIGHT RANGE
25–34 kg (55–75 lb)

HEIGHT RANGE
53–66 cm (21–26 in)

Thick, short hair is wavy, but not curly

STRAW

RED-GOLD

BROWN

BREED HISTORY Stories suggest that this breed descends from two Lesser Newfoundland puppies given to a Mr. George Law by a British army captain. These dogs were bred with local hounds to produce the Chesapeake Bay Retriever.

Small ears are set fairly high on the head and hang loosely

Wide-set, enquiring eyes

Powerful hindquarters

Toes are well rounded

AMERICAN WATER SPANIEL

The State Dog of Wisconsin, in the American Midwest, this vibrant and active breed is similar in function to the English Springer Spaniel, Brittany, and Nova Scotia Duck Tolling Retriever. It flushes or springs game from the water, and then retrieves for the hunter with its soft, retriever mouth. The dog's lean, light body allows it to accompany the hunter in his canoe or skiff, to work frigid wetland waters. Although pre-Civil War tintype photographs from the 1850s show dogs similar to this breed, it was developed to its present form during the 1920s by Dr. F.J. Pfeifer, a Wisconsin physician.

KEY FACTS

COUNTRY OF ORIGIN United States

DATE OF ORIGIN 1800s

FIRST USE Duck hunting

USE TODAY Duck hunting

LIFE EXPECTANCY 12 years

WEIGHT RANGE
11–20 kg (25–45 lb)

HEIGHT RANGE
36–46 cm (15–18 in)

*Dense coat
is tightly
curled and
covers
lively tail*

BREED HISTORY This breed probably descends, at least in part, from the Irish Water Spaniel. The Curly-coated Retriever and Field Spaniel may also have been involved in its development. The breed was first registered in 1940.

Long ears, with close curls

Upper lips hang over lower jaw

Neck blends smoothly with shoulders

Straight, strong forelegs are feathered with waterproof hair

Closely grouped toes on well-padded feet

LIVER

DARK CHOCOLATE

ENGLISH SPRINGER SPANIEL

A gundog with unlimited stamina, the English Springer thrives on physical activity, be it flushing game, or retrieving tennis balls. This leggy, powerful dog needs constant mental and physical stimulation; if these are denied, it can be quite destructive. Today, it is Great Britain's most popular working spaniel, although its bird-dog abilities were first appreciated in the United States. It is an excellent companion, and even the most urban individual probably retains sound working abilities.

KEY FACTS

COUNTRY OF ORIGIN Great Britain

DATE OF ORIGIN 1600s

FIRST USE Game flushing/ retrieving

USE TODAY Companion, gundog

LIFE EXPECTANCY 12–14 years

WEIGHT RANGE
22–24 kg (49–53 lb)

HEIGHT RANGE
48–51 cm (19–20 in)

BREED HISTORY Perhaps the root stock of all working spaniels, this breed was portrayed in paintings from the mid-1600s. It was not until the late 1800s that springers and cockers were separated into distinct breeds.

Lobe-shaped, close-set ears have excellent hair cover, and are set in line with eyes

Straight coat is firm, but not coarse

Legs feathered with long hair

BLACK/
WHITE

LIVER/
WHITE

WELSH SPRINGER SPANIEL

Hard-working, water-loving, and with outstanding stamina, the versatile Welsh Springer is an excellent companion and a superb working gundog. It has also been used as a cattle drover and sheep herder, and excels at flushing (or "springing") game birds. Unlike the English Springer, it has not diverged along separate work and show lines, although it is almost equally popular for each purpose. The breed responds well to obedience training.

Thick, silky topcoat is straight, never curly

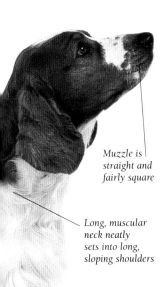

Muzzle is straight and fairly square

Dark, medium-sized eyes

Long, muscular neck neatly sets into long, sloping shoulders

Ears are smaller than an English Springer's

BREED HISTORY First depicted pictorially in the 1600s, this breed was at one time shown as the Welsh Cocker. It was recognized as a distinct breed in 1902.

KEY FACTS

COUNTRY OF ORIGIN Great Britain

DATE OF ORIGIN 1600s

FIRST USE Game retrieving/flushing

USE TODAY Companion, gundog

LIFE EXPECTANCY 12–14 years

WEIGHT RANGE
16–20 kg (35–45 lb)

HEIGHT RANGE
46–48 cm (18–19 in)

ENGLISH COCKER SPANIEL

An adept working dog, the English Cocker is also a popular household companion in both Eastern and Western Europe, and in British Commonwealth countries. Sadly, it shares with its American relative a range of inherited disorders, including numerous eye, skin, and kidney conditions, and behavioural problems, particularly rage syndrome in solid-coloured dogs. It is therefore wise to obtain details of family history before acquiring a Cocker Spaniel. Although bred primarily for companionship, the breed does well in field trials.

Slightly wavy coat, with dense, protective undercoat

VARIETY
OF
COLOURS

Long, silky hair on pendulous ears

KEY FACTS

COUNTRY OF ORIGIN Great Britain

DATE OF ORIGIN 1800s

FIRST USE Small-game retrieving

USE TODAY Companion

LIFE EXPECTANCY 13–14 years

OTHER NAME Cocker Spaniel

WEIGHT RANGE
13–15 kg (28–32 lb)

HEIGHT RANGE
38–41 cm (15–16 in)

BREED HISTORY By 1800, the small land spaniels were used as "starters", to spring game, or as "cockers", to flush and retrieve woodcock. The English Cocker descends from dogs developed in Wales and southwest England.

Back is not as short as an American Cocker's

Well-boned forelimbs

AMERICAN COCKER SPANIEL

This affectionate and most popular of all American-born breeds descends from the working English Cocker Spaniel. Although attempts have been made to work the American, and it still retains hunting instincts, its popularity lies in the gentle companionship it offers. Its beauty and charm are appreciated throughout North, Central, and South America, and also in Japan. Unfortunately, the breed suffers from a range of health problems, including epilepsy, but its generous and affable personality makes up for any physical shortcomings.

Dense, fine hair must be groomed at least daily, to prevent matting

KEY FACTS

COUNTRY OF ORIGIN United States

DATE OF ORIGIN 1800s

FIRST USE Small-game retrieving

USE TODAY Companion

LIFE EXPECTANCY 13–14 years

OTHER NAME Cocker Spaniel

WEIGHT RANGE
11–13 kg (24–28 lb)

HEIGHT RANGE
36–38 cm (14–15 in)

BREED HISTORY Legend has it that the first spaniel arrived in the United States in 1620, with the Pilgrims on the *Mayflower*. Originally, all spaniels were classified together, but eventually the American Cocker was bred for desired traits. In 1946 it was recognized as a separate breed.

Head is more distinctly domed than an English Cocker's

Slightly almond-shaped eyes

VARIETY OF COLOURS

Slightly wavy coat is silky in texture

FIELD SPANIEL

As in the case of the American Cocker Spaniel, this breed's shape changed dramatically after it was recognized as a distinct breed, with separate status from its ancestor, the English Cocker Spaniel – and in this instance, the results were disastrous. Early last century, breeders selectively bred for long backs and short, heavy-boned legs. The Field Spaniel subsequently lost all ability to perform in the field. In the 1960s, English Cocker and Springer Spaniels were used to regenerate the breed, producing today's affectionate dog.

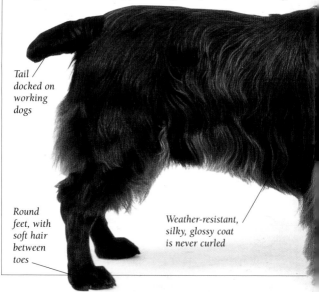

Tail docked on working dogs

Round feet, with soft hair between toes

Weather-resistant, silky, glossy coat is never curled

LIVER

BLACK

ROAN

Medium-sized eyes, with grave expression

BREED HISTORY

Originally classified as a variety of cocker spaniel, the Field Spaniel received its own recognition for show purposes in 1892. Unfortunately, breeding for the show ring led to a great deterioration in the Field Spaniel's working ability. By the end of World War II the breed was almost extinct, but by 1969 numbers had safely increased.

Low-set ears hang with graceful folds

Straight front legs, with moderately sized bones

KEY FACTS

COUNTRY OF ORIGIN Great Britain

DATE OF ORIGIN 1800s

FIRST USE Game retrieving

USE TODAY Companion

LIFE EXPECTANCY 12–13 years

WEIGHT RANGE
16–23 kg (35–50 lb)

HEIGHT RANGE
51–58 cm (20–23 in)

SUSSEX SPANIEL

Heavy but compact, with a thick skin and low-set ears, the Sussex may have evolved from dogs that were bred to work slowly over difficult terrain. A viable working dog, when it follows a scent trail it generally barks and howls, and the experienced hunter can tell what animal it is trailing from variations in the tone of its voice. One of the strong visual attractions of the Sussex is its rich, liver-coloured coat, but due to the coat's dark, dense texture, this is not a suitable breed for hot, humid environments. Selective breeding has unfortunately led to drooping lower eyelids and lower lips, conditions that can cause infections.

Coat is ample and flat, with thick, weatherproof undercoat

Legs are quite short, strong, and well feathered with hair

Feet have supportive, thick pads, and hair between toes

KEY FACTS

COUNTRY OF ORIGIN Great Britain

DATE OF ORIGIN 1800s

FIRST USE Game tracking

USE TODAY Companion

LIFE EXPECTANCY 12–13 years

WEIGHT RANGE
18–23 kg (40–50 lb)

HEIGHT RANGE
38–41 cm (15–16 in)

BREED HISTORY Its closest relatives were developed to work to the gun in dense undergrowth, but the richly coloured Sussex Spaniel was probably developed by a breeder from the county of Sussex for companionship as much as for work. With only a few individuals in North America, the breed is rare even in its home county in England.

Back is long and muscular, both in width and in depth

CLUMBER SPANIEL

According to legend, the Clumber's forebears were beaters and retrievers, owned by the French Duc de Noailles. At the time of the French Revolution, he sent a number of his dogs to the Duke of Newcastle, in England, for safety. Working Clumbers perform as a team, methodically and at a leisurely pace, beating game towards the hunters. Today, a larger proportion of the breed leads its leisurely life in urban gardens, methodically tracking and retrieving insects and fallen leaves. Although the Clumber is an avuncular animal, a bored individual can be quite destructive.

Topcoat is abundant, silky, and close

KEY FACTS

COUNTRY OF ORIGIN Great Britain

DATE OF ORIGIN 1800s

FIRST USE Tracking, game retrieving

USE TODAY Companion, tracking

LIFE EXPECTANCY 12–13 years

WEIGHT RANGE
29–36 kg (65–80 lb)

HEIGHT RANGE
48–51 cm (19–20 in)

Very powerful hind legs

BREED HISTORY Named after
Clumber Park, the Duke
of Newcastle's home in
Nottinghamshire, England,
this unique breed's ancestors
may include the Basset Hound,
resulting in its long back, and
the St. Bernard, from which it
gets its massive head.

*Large, square head
is broad on top*

*Dark-
amber
eyes*

*Large feet are
well covered
with hair*

BRITTANY

The most popular native breed in France, and the stalwart companion of hunters in Canada and the United States, the Brittany is a superb, medium-sized dog. An excellent setting and flushing gundog, the breed is often assumed to be a spaniel, much to the chagrin of its admirers, because in many countries it still carries that appellation. It may be spaniel in size, but in function it is a classic pointer, probably the world's only stumpy-tailed pointer. Rough-and-ready in appearance, the Brittany makes a trustworthy, reliable, and obedient companion.

KEY FACTS

COUNTRY OF ORIGIN France

DATE OF ORIGIN 1700s

FIRST USE Retrieving

USE TODAY Retrieving, companion

LIFE EXPECTANCY 13–14 years

OTHER NAMES Épagneul Breton, Brittany Spaniel

WEIGHT RANGE
13–15 kg (28–33 lb)

HEIGHT RANGE
46–52 cm (18–20½ in)

Haunches are well muscled

LIVER/
WHITE

BLACK/
WHITE

TRICOLOUR

Lips are tighter than those of more common spaniels

High-set, short, somewhat rounded ears

BREED HISTORY The original Brittany, as represented in old illustrations and accounts, had almost died out by the start of the 1900s, when a local breeder, Arthur Enaud, rejuvenated the breed. An affectionate and popular companion, the Brittany also hunts, points, and retrieves.

Coat is fine and dense, with sparse feathering of hair

ENGLISH SETTER

A graceful, elegant, quiet, and considerate breed, the English Setter is marvellous with children, easy to train, and a good, responsive worker in the field. There is an inherited tendency in a small number of setters to blindness, caused by a deterioration of the retinas. The predominantly white variety has a higher-than-average incidence of allergic skin conditions. This strong dog is capable of prolonged physical activity and needs a great deal of exercise.

Bright, gentle, dark-hazel eyes

Muzzle is moderately deep and square

Ears hang in neat folds, close to face

LEMON/
WHITE

BLACK/
WHITE

LIVER/
WHITE

TRICOLOUR

*Topcoat is slightly
wavy, long, and silky;
undercoat is fleecy*

KEY FACTS

COUNTRY OF ORIGIN Great Britain

DATE OF ORIGIN 1800s

FIRST USE Bird retrieving, bird setting

USE TODAY Companion, retrieving

LIFE EXPECTANCY 14 years

WEIGHT RANGE
25–30 kg (55–66 lb)

HEIGHT RANGE
61–69 cm (24–27 in)

*Straight tail tapers
to a fine point*

*Compact
feet, with
hair between
toes, are
prone to
catching
grass seeds*

BREED HISTORY Setters evolved
from spaniels, with an ability to
work as hunters. British breeder
Edward Laverack developed
today's English Setter.

GORDON SETTER

This breed is the strongest, heaviest, and slowest of the setters. It has never achieved the widespread popularity of other setters. Before hunting with guns became popular, this dog scented and found game, but then sat quietly, waiting for the hunter to arrive. This ability has contributed to the Gordon's friendly and relaxed disposition. It makes a loyal and obedient companion, but needs vigorous daily exercise.

Fairly short tail is straight and well feathered with hair

Well-arched toes are fully padded

Deep chest gives ample space for heart and lungs

Bright, dark-brown
eyes show relaxed,
but keen, expression

Broad, black
nose has
large nostrils

Lean neck
arches to head

Lips are
clearly defined

BREED HISTORY Black-
and-tan setters existed
in Great Britain in the
1600s. Today's standard
was started in the 1700s
by the Duke of Richmond
and Gordon at his home
in Banffshire, Scotland.

KEY FACTS

COUNTRY OF ORIGIN Great Britain

DATE OF ORIGIN 1600s

FIRST USE Bird setting

USE TODAY Companion, gundog

LIFE EXPECTANCY 13 years

WEIGHT RANGE
25–30 kg (56–65 lb)

HEIGHT RANGE
62–66 cm (24–26 in)

IRISH SETTER

Once known in Gaelic simply as the "Modder rhu" or "red dog", the Irish Setter was also called a red spaniel. Today, this racy, active dog thrives on physical activity. Faster than most other companion breeds, it actively seeks out other dogs to play with, perhaps because it enjoys running rings around them. The Irish Setter is an exuberant extrovert. Its late maturing, and joy of life, give it an undeserved reputation for being flighty and overly excitable.

Silky coat is long; undercoat is abundant in cold weather

Tail set low, carried horizontally or down

Nose is black or chocolate coloured

Oval eyes have gentle expression

KEY FACTS

COUNTRY OF ORIGIN Ireland

DATE OF ORIGIN 1700s

FIRST USE Game retrieving, setting

USE TODAY Companion

LIFE EXPECTANCY 13 years

OTHER NAMES Irish Red Setter, Red Setter

WEIGHT RANGE
27–32 kg (60–70 lb)

HEIGHT RANGE
64–69 cm (25–27 in)

BREED HISTORY The Old Spanish Pointer (not known outside Spain), setting spaniels, and early Scottish setters have been included in the Irish Setter's evolution.

Sinewy forelegs, and small feet

IRISH RED-AND-WHITE SETTER

Just like its Irish Setter relative, the Red-and-white takes more time to obedience train than most other gundogs, but once trained it makes a reliable companion. Its zest for life leads it to injure itself more frequently than calmer breeds. The deep chest makes this setter prone to gastric torsion, an intense and sudden twisting of the stomach – a life-and-death emergency. The breed has a refined sense of smell, and if worked, is an enthusiastic and effective gundog.

Fairly deep muzzle

KEY FACTS

COUNTRY OF ORIGIN Ireland

DATE OF ORIGIN 1700s

FIRST USE Game retrieving, setting

USE TODAY Companion, gundog

LIFE EXPECTANCY 13 years

WEIGHT RANGE
27–32 kg (60–70 lb)

HEIGHT RANGE
58–69 cm (23–27 in)

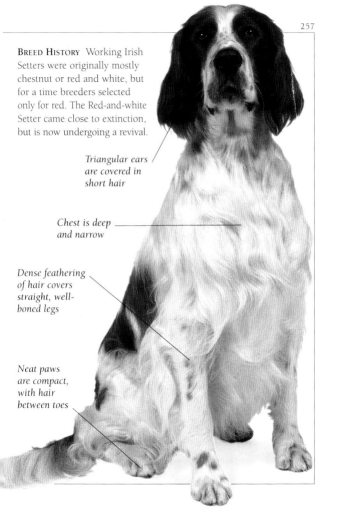

BREED HISTORY Working Irish Setters were originally mostly chestnut or red and white, but for a time breeders selected only for red. The Red-and-white Setter came close to extinction, but is now undergoing a revival.

Triangular ears are covered in short hair

Chest is deep and narrow

Dense feathering of hair covers straight, well-boned legs

Neat paws are compact, with hair between toes

ENGLISH POINTER

Gentle, obedient, and with a tendency to take life rather seriously, the English Pointer's original purpose contradicted natural dog behaviour. Upon sighting a hare it would stand and point, permitting accompanying greyhounds to chase and seize the animal. Selective breeding has created an intensely biddable, noble, and giving individual, but one that is overly sensitive. The Pointer's kindly disposition makes it an ideal family companion.

Thighs are lean and well muscled

KEY FACTS

COUNTRY OF ORIGIN Great Britain

DATE OF ORIGIN 1600s

FIRST USE Game tracking

USE TODAY Companion, gundog

LIFE EXPECTANCY 13–14 years

OTHER NAME Pointer

WEIGHT RANGE
20–30 kg (44–66 lb)

HEIGHT RANGE
61–69 cm (24–27 in)

Oval feet have arched toes and well-cushioned pads

Well-defined depression before the eyes separates dome of skull from muzzle

High-set ears hang loose, even when dog is alert

Straight line extends from long, sloping shoulders to lower forelegs

Fine, smooth, hard coat, with good sheen

BREED HISTORY

Although its exact origins are unclear, the English Pointer was developed wholly in Great Britain. At some stage in its development, lines from the now-extinct Old Spanish Setter were probably used.

LEMON/ WHITE

ORANGE/ WHITE

LIVER/ WHITE

BLACK/ WHITE

GERMAN POINTERS

Today's German Pointers have a variety of origins, but all of them are a result of intense dog-breeding programmes in Germany in the late 1800s. Using national blood stock, as well as French and British breeding lines, three distinct pointers were created. The Wire-haired is a marvellous family dog, as well as a hardy worker. Hip and elbow arthritis are inherited conditions in the breed, but with careful selection can be avoided. Long-haired Pointers remain primarily working dogs. Some may be timid, but virtually all are excellent companions and good watchdogs. The Short-haired can also be timid, and seizures have been a problem in some lines. However, the breed is longer-lived than most other dogs of its size, and makes an amenable companion.

KEY FACTS

COUNTRY OF ORIGIN Germany

DATE OF ORIGIN 1800s

FIRST USE General hunting

USE TODAY Companion, gundog

LIFE EXPECTANCY 12–14 years

OTHER NAME Deutscher Drahthaariger Vorstehhund

WEIGHT RANGE
27–32 kg (60–70 lb)

HEIGHT RANGE
60–65 cm (24–26 in)

LIVER/ WHITE

BLACK

BLACK/ WHITE

LIVER

Feet are robust

BREED HISTORY Until the 1800s, German Pointers were heavy, tranquil, and slow. Crossing these saddle-backed, rabbit-footed dogs with the lighter English Pointer produced today's lean, athletic, and responsive breed. The German Short-haired has become a favourite with hunters in Germany and Great Britain, and with field-trial enthusiasts in North America.

Moderately long, high-set ears

Close-fitting eyelids

Short, thick, hard coat is harsh to the touch

Chest is deeper than it is broad, and covered with well-sprung ribs

Long, straight forelegs, with solid bone and close-fitting skin

Thighs are broad, well muscled, and lean

GERMAN SHORT-HAIRED POINTER

BREED HISTORY Developed as an all-purpose flusher, pointer, and retriever, the Wire-haired is a combination of Short-haired Pointer, French Wire-haired Pointing Griffon, German Pudelpointer (a rare poodle/pointer cross), and Broken-coated Pointer (now extinct). The breed was first recognized in Germany in 1870.

Robust, coarse beard

GERMAN WIRE-HAIRED POINTER

LIVER/ WHITE

BLACK/ WHITE

LIVER

Tail is profusely feathered with hair

GERMAN LONG-HAIRED POINTER

BREED HISTORY The German Long-haired Pointer owes its looks and temperament in part to a variety of long-haired continental bird dogs. Cross breeding with Irish and Gordon Setters produced red-and-black coloration, but this is generally not accepted for registration. The Long-haired made its first public appearance in Hanover, Germany, in 1879.

Long, lean head, with well-spaced, gentle-looking eyes

Wide, long muzzle with brown nose

Broad-based ears are covered with wavy hair

Prominent chest

Long, straight forelegs are well fringed with soft hair

Moderately round feet have thick hair between toes

LARGE MUNSTERLANDER

The Large Munsterlander's survival was based more upon negatives than positives. As the German Long-haired Pointer declined, a breed club was formed to save that breed, adopting as its standard only liver-and-white specimens. However, hunters in the Münster region of Germany, interested in both form and function, continued to breed from black-and-white dogs that appeared in litters. The Large Munsterlander thrives on companionship.

KEY FACTS

COUNTRY OF ORIGIN Germany

DATE OF ORIGIN 1800s

FIRST USE Tracking, pointing, retrieving

USE TODAY Companion, gundog

LIFE EXPECTANCY 12–13 years

OTHER NAME Grosser Münsterländer Vorstehhund

WEIGHT RANGE
25–29 kg (55–65 lb)

HEIGHT RANGE
59–61 cm (23–24 in)

Tail is in line with back, and is well feathered with hair

BREED HISTORY Descended from German bird dogs, this breed began as the black-and-white colour variation of the liver-and-white German Long-haired Pointer. In 1919 its breed club was formed, and like its smaller relative, the Small Munsterlander, it is becoming increasingly popular outside Germany.

Broad, round-tipped ears hang close to head

Muscular neck

Long, dense coat is neither coarse nor curly

Plenty of hair on long, straight forelegs

Firm, strong feet, with black-nailed toes

CZESKY FOUSEK

This responsive dog is one of Bohemia's most popular hunting dogs. A multi-purpose worker, it points, sets, and then retrieves from land or water. At ease in the home, it is almost always amenable with children. There can be a dramatic difference in size between the sexes – the largest males can be almost 50 per cent bigger than the smallest females. Some individuals can be particularly headstrong and need firm control. With regular exercise, this breed makes an attractive, amenable companion, although it is best suited to the countryside. First bred to written standards in the late 1800s, the excellent Czesky Fousek deserves recognition outside its native land.

Tail is set to lengthen back

Coat has soft, dense undercoat, and hard, rough topcoat

Spoon-shaped feet, with strong, dark nails

KEY FACTS

COUNTRY OF ORIGIN Czech Republic

DATE OF ORIGIN 1800s

FIRST USE Game pointing

USE TODAY Game pointing, companion

LIFE EXPECTANCY 12–13 years

OTHER NAMES Czech Pointer, Czech Coarse-haired Setter

WEIGHT RANGE
22–34 kg (48½–75 lb)

HEIGHT RANGE
58–66 cm (23–26 in)

High-set ears are broad at base and pointed towards tips

Muzzle is slightly longer than skull

Strong, well-muscled elbows on straight, lean legs

BREED HISTORY It is possible that ancestors of the Czesky Fousek were pointing and setting wildfowl in the 1400s. Last century, the breed was reconstituted with the infusion of German Wire-haired and Short-haired Pointer bloodlines.

BROWN/
WHITE

BROWN

WIRE-HAIRED POINTING GRIFFON

Eduard Korthals never revealed the breeds he used to develop the Wire-haired Pointing Griffon, but it is likely that the Munsterlander, German Short-haired Pointer, and French griffons (rough-coated scent hounds) all played roles. This all-terrain, all-weather, all-game pointer-retriever was the first general-purpose European gundog to be formally recognized in the United States. It is responsive, obedient, good with children, not snappy, and usually easygoing with other dogs, although males can be aggressive.

Thigh muscles are well developed

KEY FACTS

COUNTRY OF ORIGIN France

DATE OF ORIGIN 1860s

FIRST USE Hunting, retrieving

USE TODAY Hunting, retrieving, companion

LIFE EXPECTANCY 12–13 years

OTHER NAME Griffon d'Arrêt Korthals

WEIGHT RANGE
23–27 kg (50–60 lb)

HEIGHT RANGE
56–61 cm (22–24 in)

Bushy eyebrows
cover large,
yellow-brown eyes

Skull is long and
narrow, with
square muzzle

Beard of
long, thick,
harsh hair

Forelimbs are
straight and
long, with wispy
feathering of hair

BREED HISTORY A classic
"Euro-dog", this breed
was developed from
Dutch, Belgian, German,
French, and possibly
English gundogs by a
Dutch breeder, Eduard
Korthals, who lived in
both the Netherlands
and Germany. This
versatile gundog remains
uncommon in Europe
and North America.

HUNGARIAN VIZSLA

Elegant and gentle, but energetic, the Hungarian Vizsla probably would not have survived World War II, had not Hungarian expatriates taken their favoured companions with them when they emigrated to other parts of Europe and North America in the 1930s. The Vizsla's original dual purpose, pointing and retrieving, has been extended to a third purpose in the last 20 years – that of a widely admired family companion, which is obedient, reliable, and healthy. The breed is becoming increasingly popular in Hungary, and its original purpose has not been forgotten. In Canada, the wire-haired variety is commonly seen at work as a gundog with weekend hunters. It has a good nose, follows trails diligently, and retrieves either game or thrown tennis balls with enthusiasm.

KEY FACTS

COUNTRY OF ORIGIN Hungary

DATE OF ORIGIN Middle Ages/1930s

FIRST USE Hunting, falconry

USE TODAY Companion, gundog

LIFE EXPECTANCY 14–15 years

OTHER NAMES Magyar Vizsla, Drotszoru Magyar Vizsla

WEIGHT RANGE
22–30 kg (48½–66 lb)

HEIGHT RANGE
57–64 cm (22½–25 in)

On short-haired variety, coat is short, smooth, dense, shiny, and lies close to body; only wire-haired has undercoat

Elbows are close on straight, strong, muscular forelimbs

Thin, silky ears have rounded tips, and hang close to cheeks

Chest is moderately deep, reaching down to elbows

BREED HISTORY The name was first used in 1510 to describe the result of crossing two now-extinct breeds, the indigenous Pannonian Hound and the Yellow Turkish Dog. Today's short-haired gundog was established by the 1850s. The wire-haired variety was developed in the 1930s.

WEIMARANER

Rippling with muscles, this gundog is popular both as a tracker-retriever and as a companion. The Weimaraner usually has an alert, obedient, and fearless personality, although timidity is not unknown in the breed. Both the popular short-haired and less common long-haired versions are proficient in field trials, obedience work, and hunting, and make reliable watchdogs. The breed has grace, speed, strength, stamina, and undeniable "star quality", with its handsome carriage and shimmering steel coat colour. Easy to obedience train, it is equally at home in towns or rural areas.

Arresting eyes have unusual colour, from amber to grey to blue

Short-haired variety has sleek, smooth coat

Feet are compact

BREED HISTORY Named after the sport-loving court of Charles August, Grand Duke of Weimar, this magnificent breed's exact origins are unknown, although its root stock could come from the now-extinct Leithund. Selective breeding in the 1800s resulted in today's standard.

High-set ears are slightly folded

Neat lips meet brown nose

Aristocratic head, with long muzzle and skull

Deep chest, with well-sprung ribs and powerful shoulders

Forelegs are straight and strong

KEY FACTS

COUNTRY OF ORIGIN Germany

DATE OF ORIGIN 1600s

FIRST USE Large-game tracking

USE TODAY Gundog, companion

LIFE EXPECTANCY 12–13 years

OTHER NAME Weimaraner Vorstehhund

WEIGHT RANGE
32–39 kg (70½–86 lb)

HEIGHT RANGE
56–69 cm (22–27 in)

BRACCO ITALIANO

Extremely fashionable in Renaissance Italy, this energetic, sensible, but slightly stubborn breed then declined in popularity. It was recently "rediscovered", first by Italian dog breeders, and then by breeders elsewhere in the European Union. Today, this powerful and well-proportioned dog is a common sight at major European dog shows. Serious, but with a gentle air, it makes a sensitive companion. This unique-looking breed is also a vigorous hunter, capable of scenting, pointing, and retrieving both on land and in water.

WHITE

WHITE/
ORANGE,
WHITE/
CHESTNUT

KEY FACTS

COUNTRY OF ORIGIN Italy

DATE OF ORIGIN 1700s

FIRST USE Tracking, pointing, retrieving

USE TODAY Companion, gundog

LIFE EXPECTANCY 12–13 years

OTHER NAMES Italian Pointer, Italian Setter

WEIGHT RANGE
25–40 kg (55–88 lb)

HEIGHT RANGE
56–67 cm (22–26½ in)

Moderate bend to hocks below quite long thighs

BREED HISTORY Some say that this breed, which evolved in Piedmont and Lombardy, Italy, is the result of crosses between the Segugio and an ancient Asiatic mastiff. Others claim that it descends from the St. Hubert Jura Hound, a Swiss mountain dog.

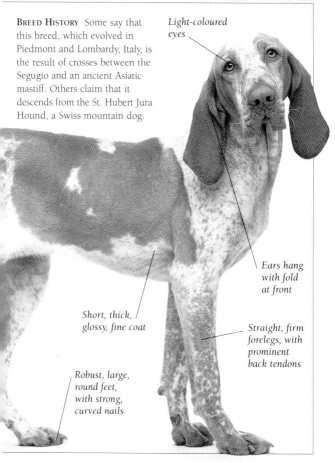

Light-coloured eyes

Ears hang with fold at front

Short, thick, glossy, fine coat

Straight, firm forelegs, with prominent back tendons

Robust, large, round feet, with strong, curved nails

ITALIAN SPINONE

The Italian Spinone has recently found popularity far beyond its native land. Rightly so. It may produce a little more tenacious saliva than some people are willing to cope with, and it may have a rather pungent canine aroma, but otherwise this is an avuncular, calm, easygoing, and obedient breed that thrives on work, be it hunting, field trials, or chasing bouncing dog toys. Although the Spinone looks dignified, reserved, and all-knowing, it is, in its ambling way, actively playful, even rowdy.

Triangular ears, with short, thick hair

Coat is thick, rough, close fitting, and slightly wiry

KEY FACTS

COUNTRY OF ORIGIN Italy

DATE OF ORIGIN Middle Ages

FIRST USE Game retrieving

USE TODAY Companion, field trials, gundog

LIFE EXPECTANCY 12–13 years

OTHER NAMES Spinone Italiano, Spinone

WEIGHT RANGE
32–37 kg (71–82 lb)

HEIGHT RANGE
61–66 cm (24–26 in)

WHITE

WHITE/ ORANGE, WHITE/ CHESTNUT

BREED HISTORY The Spinone could be descended from the Segugio, or perhaps the now-extinct Korthal Griffon. Its present form developed in Piedmont and Lombardy, Italy, and was apparent by the 1200s. Appealing in both looks and character, this breed should become increasingly popular.

Long hair on moustache and beard

Straight forelegs are densely boned, with distinct back tendons

Long, broad, muscular thighs have slight arch at back

LIVESTOCK DOGS

Guarding a person's campsite or homestead is natural behaviour for a dog. In the delta between the Tigris and Euphrates rivers, in what is now Iraq, where our hunter ancestors became cultivators and farmers, dogs were also used to protect livestock. It was found that dogs raised from puppyhood with sheep, goats, or cattle would defend them as members of their own pack. These guardians soon proved indispensable.

ANCIENT ROOTS

Flocks and herds of livestock were originally small, and could easily be protected as a group from wolves and thieves. As the number of animals increased, small, agile dogs were used to move strays back to the herd – these became herders. As shepherds began to transport their animals over long distances, another group of dogs evolved, the drovers. These both protected livestock and moved them along. Bulky drovers developed to move cattle, while smaller, more agile drovers developed to move sheep and goats. These smaller drovers were the forerunners of the modern sheepdog.

Through selective breeding, the mastiff was produced to protect flocks and property that followed armies. These massive dogs spread throughout Europe, and many of today's mountain dogs are descended from mastiffs. Cattle-guarding mastiffs accompanied Roman legions 2,000 years ago across the Alps to Switzerland, leaving behind the ancestors of the Swiss mountain dogs. In Rome, mastiffs fought either

German Shepherd Dog

against other animals or among themselves in the gladiator's ring. Their descendants became bull and bear baiters and fighting dogs, although their main duty remained protecting the home. Bullmastiffs, bulldogs, the Great Dane, and Boxer descend from this source. Exported to South America, fighting dogs provided the main stock for local mastiffs.

Beauceron

GUARDIANS AND HERDERS

Livestock guarding remained a primary responsibility of mastiff-type dogs, but cattle and pig farmers and butchers required robust, agile dogs to both protect and move livestock. The Old English Sheepdog was once an excellent cattle drover. So, too, were the Corgi and Swedish Vallhund. In Germany, the Giant and Standard Schnauzers and the Rottweiler filled this role, while in France today the Bouvier des Flandres excels as a cattle mover. In Australia, the Australian Cattle Dog and a variety of heelers still work large herds of cattle. Other, more strictly defensive, guardian breeds spread from Asia into Europe and Africa. A variety of sheepdogs developed in the Balkans, while in Hungary the Komondor still guards and protects. Further into Europe,

other huge guardians, such as the Kuvasz and Maremma (always white to differentiate them from marauding wolves and to bond them to their flocks), would patrol their fiefdoms, guarding but not herding. To help control their large flocks, shepherds also used herders such as the Bergamasco and Polish Lowland Sheepdog. The herding shepherd dog continued to evolve, probably from guarding breeds. In Great Britain, this produced the superb collies. Elsewhere in northern Europe, sheep herders evolved in Belgium, the Netherlands, France, and Germany – all bred for proficiency at herding and obedience. The versatile German Shepherd is now used for a diverse range of activities.

HELPFUL ROLE

Guarding and herding breeds vary in looks and temperament, but all share a background in protecting and assisting.

Lancashire Heeler

GERMAN SHEPHERD DOG

It may well be that the German Shepherd Dog, and its close Dutch and Belgian shepherd relatives, have existed in much today's form for thousands of years. By the beginning of World War I, the German Shepherd was popular throughout Germany, and swiftly spread to other parts of the world. Indiscriminate breeding has, unfortunately, produced both physical and behavioural problems. Arthritis of the joints, eye disease, gastrointestinal disease, and other medical problems occur frequently. Equally common are timidity, fearfulness, nervousness, and aggression to other dogs. When bred carefully, however, this is an excellent breed – reliable, calm, responsive, and obedient.

Thighs are strong and muscular, with leg bones carried slightly flexed

Small, arched, round feet

Erect, high-set ears give impression of alertness

Upper part of head narrows gradually from eyes to nose

Chest is deep

VARIETY OF COLOURS

BREED HISTORY The world's most numerous breed has its recent origins in the superlative breeding programme which Max von Stephanitz began at the end of the 1800s. Using long-haired, short-haired, and wire-haired shepherd dogs from Bavaria, Wurtemberg, and Thurginia, breeders produced the obedient, handsome German Shepherd Dog. Today, in most countries, only the short coat is recognized for show purposes.

KEY FACTS

COUNTRY OF ORIGIN Germany

DATE OF ORIGIN 1800s

FIRST USE Sheep herding

USE TODAY Companion, security, assistance

LIFE EXPECTANCY 12–13 years

OTHER NAMES Alsatian, Deutscher Schaferhund

WEIGHT RANGE
34–43 kg (75–95 lb)

HEIGHT RANGE
55–66 cm (22–26 in)

GROENENDAEL

Classifying the Belgian shepherds is not easy because national kennel clubs cannot agree on how to name them. In 1891, Professor Adolphe Reul, of the Belgian School of Veterinary Science, conducted a field study of all the existing sheepdogs in Belgium, and eventually four different breeds came to be recognized nationally. In many countries, these are classified as varieties of one breed, the Belgian Shepherd. In the United States, however, the Groenendael is the Belgian Shepherd, while the Malinois and Tervueren are recognized separately, and the Laekenois not at all. All share an extremely robust personality and need early training.

Triangular, rigid ears

Long, smooth, black hair, especially abundant around shoulders, neck, and chest

BREED HISTORY At the end of the 1800s, breeders took an active interest in native sheepdogs, and standards were set to stabilize them into as few breeds as possible. Belgium originally recognized eight standards, including the Groenendael, which was developed by a Belgian breeder, Nicholas Rose.

KEY FACTS

COUNTRY OF ORIGIN Belgium

DATE OF ORIGIN Middle Ages/1800s

FIRST USE Livestock herding

USE TODAY Companion, watchdog

LIFE EXPECTANCY 13–14 years

OTHER NAMES Chien de Berger Belge, Belgian Shepherd, Belgian Sheepdog

WEIGHT RANGE
27.5–28.5 kg (61–63 lb)

HEIGHT RANGE
56–66 cm (22–26 in)

Tail is of moderate length, and well feathered with hair

LAEKENOIS

Although it is as strong willed and opinionated as its three close relatives, this breed is less inclined to snap than the Groenendael, Malinois, and Tervueren. The relative rarity of the Laekenois is inexplicable – it is just as fertile, and as capable a working dog, as the other Belgian shepherds, although its rustic looks may put off potential breeders. Ever alert and highly active, it responds well to obedience training and makes an excellent watchdog. It is good with children if it is introduced to them at an early age, but it can sometimes be troublesome with other dogs.

Hindquarters are muscular, without looking heavy

Dense hair is bushy on tail, but not particularly long

Fawn-coloured coat is harsh, dry, and normally slightly tangled

High-set,
stiff ears

Bristly
muzzle

KEY FACTS

COUNTRY OF ORIGIN Belgium

DATE OF ORIGIN Middle Ages/1800s

FIRST USE Livestock herding/
guarding

USE TODAY Companion, watchdog

LIFE EXPECTANCY 12–14 years

OTHER NAMES Laekense, Chien de
Berger Belge (see also Groenendael)

WEIGHT RANGE
27.5–28.5 kg (61–63 lb)

HEIGHT RANGE
56–66 cm (22–26 in)

BREED HISTORY Today the rarest
of the four remaining Belgian
shepherds, the rough, shaggy-
coated Laekenois, favoured dog
of Queen Henrietta of Belgium,
is named after the Château de
Laeken, a residence she often
visited. The breed was first
recognized in 1897, and is
similar to the rough-haired
variety of the related
Dutch Shepherd.

MALINOIS

The Malinois has a coat similar to that of the smooth-haired variety of the related Dutch Shepherd, but its temperament is closest to that of the Laekenois – active and alert, with an instinct to guard and protect. After the Laekenois, this is the least popular of the Belgian shepherds, although both of these breeds are possibly less snappy than the Tervueren and Groenendael. Its rareness could be due to the fact that it is competing with the popular German Shepherd, which it closely resembles. The Malinois is, however, a resourceful dog, and police forces are increasingly using it for security work.

Chest is not wide, but it is deep and roomy

Forelegs are held close to body

BREED HISTORY The first of the Belgian shepherds to establish type, the Malinois became the gauge by which other Belgian sheepdogs were judged. It is named after the area of Malines, where this form of sheepdog was most populous. Its conformation is closest to the German Shepherd's.

KEY FACTS

COUNTRY OF ORIGIN Belgium

DATE OF ORIGIN Middle Ages/1800s

FIRST USE Livestock herding

USE TODAY Companion, security, assistance

LIFE EXPECTANCY 12–14 years

OTHER NAMES see Groenendael

WEIGHT RANGE
27.5–28.5 kg (61–63 lb)

HEIGHT RANGE
56–66 cm (22–26 in)

Short, hard, fawn-coloured hairs are tipped with black

When relaxed, tail hangs limp, with slight curl to last quarter

GREY

FAWN

RED

TERVUEREN

The Tervueren's trainability and ability to concentrate have made it a favourite for agility trials, police and security service work, and assistance work with blind or disabled people. One of the success stories of the last 10 years has been the use of the breed as a scent detector – it finds drugs as they are smuggled across national borders. The Tervueren's long, double-pigmented coat, in which each light-coloured hair has a black tip, adds to its appeal, and is partly responsible for its growing popularity. Like all the Belgian shepherds, this breed thrives when it is controlled by a firm and understanding hand.

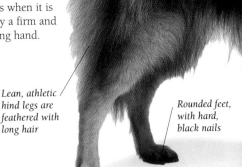

GREY

FAWN

RED

Lean, athletic hind legs are feathered with long hair

Rounded feet, with hard, black nails

Ruff of long hair circles neck and hides dense undercoat

BREED HISTORY In temperament and looks closest to the Groenendael (Groenendael matings occasionally produce Tervueren puppies), this breed descends from the stock that created the Groenendael. Near extinction by the end of World War II, in the last decade it has surged in popularity, especially as a drug-detecting dog.

KEY FACTS

COUNTRY OF ORIGIN Belgium

DATE OF ORIGIN Middle Ages/1800s

FIRST USE Livestock herding

USE TODAY Companion, security, assistance

LIFE EXPECTANCY 12–14 years

OTHER NAMES see Groenendael

WEIGHT RANGE
27.5–28.5 kg (61–63 lb)

HEIGHT RANGE
56–66 cm (22–26 in)

BORDER COLLIE

Still the most popular working sheepdog in Great Britain and Ireland, the Border can make an affectionate but difficult pet, especially in cities. Border Collies from working lines have a strong predatory instinct, which is channelled through breeding and training into a superb herding ability. Without constant stimulation, this need to work will vent itself in destructive behaviour, such as herding other dogs or people, or snappiness.

KEY FACTS

COUNTRY OF ORIGIN Great Britain

DATE OF ORIGIN 1700s

FIRST USE Sheep/cattle herding

USE TODAY Companion, sheep herding, sheepdog trials

LIFE EXPECTANCY 12–14 years

WEIGHT RANGE
14–22 kg (30–49 lb)

HEIGHT RANGE
46–54 cm (18–21 in)

Fairly large, wide-set eyes; muzzle tapers and is slightly blunt

BREED HISTORY Although shepherds in the hilly Scottish Borders used collies for many years, this breed was not given its present name until 1915.

RED

BLUE-
MERLE

BLACK/
WHITE

TRICOLOUR

BROWN

BLACK

*Dense, slightly
harsh, but
shiny, topcoat*

*Mane is
quite heavy*

*Tail carried low,
but with an up-
swirl at tip*

*Well-boned,
straight
forelimbs*

ROUGH COLLIE

The Rough Collie's elegant good looks first attracted the attention of breeders, and then the public. After Queen Victoria acquired the breed as a companion, its popularity increased, but it was not until Hollywood discovered it and produced the Lassie films that international recognition and popularity were assured. The breed's success in the show ring has tended to override its original herding abilities. It is an excellent companion, a good watchdog, easy to obedience train, and safe with, and extremely protective of, children. Its coat mats easily, and needs daily grooming.

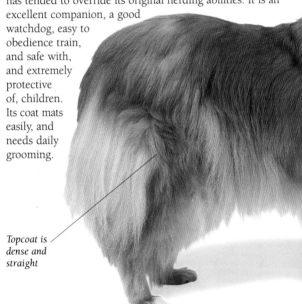

Topcoat is dense and straight

Head resembles a blunted wedge

SABLE/
WHITE

BLUE-
MERLE

TRICOLOUR

Abundant, smooth, shiny mane

Almond-shaped, slightly oblique eyes

Nose is prone to sunburn

BREED HISTORY
Originating in its present form in the cold regions of northern Scotland, the working Rough Collie was shorter in leg and nose than today's elegant breed.

Fringe of long hair on forelegs

KEY FACTS

COUNTRY OF ORIGIN Great Britain

DATE OF ORIGIN 1800s

FIRST USE Sheep herding

USE TODAY Companion

LIFE EXPECTANCY 12–14 years

OTHER NAME Scottish Collie

WEIGHT RANGE
18–30 kg (40–66 lb)

HEIGHT RANGE
51–61 cm (20–24 in)

SMOOTH COLLIE

For most of its history, the Smooth Collie has been classified with the Rough, since that breed occasionally gives birth to smooth-coated puppies. The personalities of the two breeds have, however, diverged, perhaps because of the smaller gene pool of the rather uncommon Smooth Collie. Not as popular as the Rough, it is very rare outside Great Britain, and has a greater tendency to be shy and snappy. Nevertheless, the Smooth Collie makes a good companion, and is suited to life in the city.

Muscular thighs; legs are sinewy below thighs

Coat is short and dense

SABLE/
WHITE

BLUE-
MERLE

TRICOLOUR

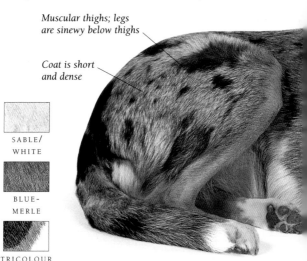

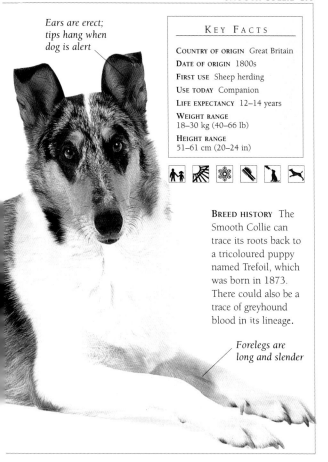

*Ears are erect;
tips hang when
dog is alert*

KEY FACTS

COUNTRY OF ORIGIN Great Britain

DATE OF ORIGIN 1800s

FIRST USE Sheep herding

USE TODAY Companion

LIFE EXPECTANCY 12–14 years

WEIGHT RANGE
18–30 kg (40–66 lb)

HEIGHT RANGE
51–61 cm (20–24 in)

BREED HISTORY The
Smooth Collie can
trace its roots back to
a tricoloured puppy
named Trefoil, which
was born in 1873.
There could also be a
trace of greyhound
blood in its lineage.

*Forelegs are
long and slender*

SHETLAND SHEEPDOG

The Sheltie is consistently one of the most popular breeds in Japan, and is also popular in Great Britain and North America. Although it is rarely used as a working dog, it retains many of its guarding and herding instincts, and will efficiently protect its owner's home. Although once called the Dwarf Scotch Shepherd, the breed is a classic miniature, not a dwarf like a dachshund. It is a smaller version of the large working sheepdogs of Scotland. Miniaturization has brought with it an increased risk of fractures to long, thin leg bones, and a rather high incidence of inherited digestive problems and eye conditions.

SABLE

TRICOLOUR

BLUE-MERLE

BLACK/TAN

BLACK/WHITE

Long, harsh topcoat

Small, semi-erect ears are close set

BREED HISTORY This breed may be the result of crossing imported Rough Collies with dogs from the Scottish Shetland Islands.

Head tapers elegantly from ears to nose

Abundant frill of long hair around neck

KEY FACTS

COUNTRY OF ORIGIN Great Britain

DATE OF ORIGIN 1700s

FIRST USE Sheep herding

USE TODAY Companion, sheep herding

LIFE EXPECTANCY 12–14 years

WEIGHT RANGE
6–7 kg (14–16 lb)

HEIGHT RANGE
35–37 cm (14–15 in)

BEARDED COLLIE

Exuberance is the cardinal personality trait of this ancient breed. Having almost disappeared as a working dog, it was revived in 1944 when Mrs. Willison, owner of Jeannie, acquired Bailie, who she saw playing on an English beach. Virtually all of today's Beardies descend from these two dogs. This high-spirited, friendly breed needs constant mental and physical stimulation, and is ideal for people with time and energy.

KEY FACTS

COUNTRY OF ORIGIN Great Britain

DATE OF ORIGIN 1500s

FIRST USE Sheep herding

USE TODAY Companion

LIFE EXPECTANCY 12–13 years

OTHER NAME Beardie

WEIGHT RANGE
18–27 kg (40–60 lb)

HEIGHT RANGE
51–56 cm (20–22 in)

Drooping ears are lost under long hair

Forelegs are covered with long, shaggy hair

BREED HISTORY Mythically, the Bearded Collie has Polish Lowland Sheepdog origins. After conquering Great Britain, it successfully colonized the United States and Canada.

GREY

FAWN

BLUE

BROWN

BLACK

Long body has level back; hair naturally parts down middle

Low-set, long tail is abundantly feathered with hair

OLD ENGLISH SHEEPDOG

In 1961, a British paint manufacturer launched television advertisements, using the Old English Sheepdog as its symbol. Sales of this breed subsequently increased as rapidly as did the manufacturer's paint sales. Its old, aggressive instincts occasionally rise to the surface – however, early training is necessary more to control the breed's intense demands for affection. Although this burly dog is capable of behaving like the proverbial bull in a china shop, it is an excellent companion and guard.

Coat becomes harder and shaggier as puppy grows to adult

KEY FACTS

COUNTRY OF ORIGIN Great Britain

DATE OF ORIGIN 1800s

FIRST USE Sheep herding

USE TODAY Companion

LIFE EXPECTANCY 12–13 years

OTHER NAME Bobtail

WEIGHT RANGE
29.5–30.5 kg (65–67 lb)

HEIGHT RANGE
56–61 cm (22–24 in)

BLUE   GREY

BREED HISTORY The Old English probably traces its origins back to continental sheepdogs, such as the Briard. Selective breeding began in the 1880s.

Almost square head has long, strong, square, truncated jaws

Shoulders are lower than loins when dog is standing

Profuse coat, with waterproof undercoat

CARDIGAN WELSH CORGI

Watch your ankles when you are near a Cardigan Welsh Corgi. This robust working dog is an instinctive "heeler", which originally drove livestock by nipping at its heels; it was built low enough to the ground to avoid flailing hooves. *Cur* once meant to watch over, and in old Welsh, *gi* means dog. The Corgi lives up to its name – it is a watchful and snappy defender of property, and drover of sheep and cattle. It also makes an exuberant companion.

KEY FACTS

COUNTRY OF ORIGIN Great Britain

DATE OF ORIGIN Middle Ages?

FIRST USE Livestock drover

USE TODAY Companion, livestock drover

LIFE EXPECTANCY 12–14 years

WEIGHT RANGE
11–17 kg (25–38 lb)

HEIGHT RANGE
27–32 cm (10½–12½ in)

Smooth, protective topcoat covers soft, insulating undercoat

Fox-like brush tail

ANY
COLOUR

Dark, medium-sized, slightly oblique eyes are set wide apart

Powerful and slightly arched neck on sloping shoulders

BREED HISTORY Some authorities say that this breed arrived in Great Britain with the Celts over 3,000 years ago. Others say that it is a distant relative of continental bassets and reached Great Britain just over 1,000 years ago. In the 1800s, cross breeding with the Pembroke Welsh Corgi reduced the differences between the two breeds.

PEMBROKE WELSH CORGI

The Pembroke Welsh Corgi bears a striking resemblance to the Swedish Vallhund. It is possible that the Vikings took ancestors of this determined little heeler back to Scandinavia from their settlements in Great Britain. Until the 1800s, heelers were used extensively throughout Great Britain to drive cattle to markets. The stamina and efficiency of the Pembroke's ancestors made it a popular working dog. Although the breed is still worked today, most Pembrokes are kept as companions. Breeders have been moderately successful in reducing the inclination of this breed to nip.

Lack of tail is an inherited trait

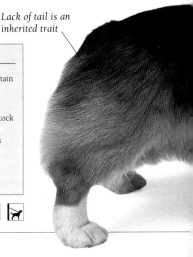

KEY FACTS

COUNTRY OF ORIGIN Great Britain

DATE OF ORIGIN 900s

FIRST USE Livestock drover

USE TODAY Companion, livestock drover

LIFE EXPECTANCY 12–14 years

WEIGHT RANGE
10–12 kg (20–26 lb)

HEIGHT RANGE
25–31 cm (10–12 in)

SABLE

FAWN

BLACK/
TAN

RED

Erect, firm ears have rounded tips

BREED HISTORY Ancient records indicate that the Pembroke Welsh Corgi has existed in Great Britain since at least AD 920. One story tells that the breed accompanied Flemish weavers brought to Great Britain by King Henry I of England.

Body is significantly shorter than that of a Cardigan

LANCASHIRE HEELER

With the advent of mechanized transport, the work of the old heeler breeds was no longer necessary. In Great Britain, the Yorkshire and Norfolk Heelers, the Drover's Cur, and London's Smithfield Collie all became extinct. Today's Lancashire Heeler, although in colour (black with tan markings) and size almost identical to its ancient namesake, is seldom used as a cattle dog, and has never learned to act like one. It has the alertness and rat- and rabbit-catching potential of its terrier parentage, and makes a pleasant companion.

Tail is set high and carried forwards over back

BREED HISTORY Heelers, which drove livestock by nipping their heels, were common wherever cattle were walked to market. The Lancashire Heeler became extinct in the early 1900s. Today's breed, which is a 1960s' recreation, is largely a cross between the Welsh Corgi and Manchester Terrier.

Hindquarters are very well muscled

Legs are short in relation to body size

*Large, bright eyes
are set wide apart*

*Muzzle fur is first
area to change
colour with age*

*Long, deep chest
and abdomen below
firm, strong back*

*Forepaws are
covered in tan-
coloured fur,
and turn
out slightly*

KEY FACTS

COUNTRY OF ORIGIN Great Britain

DATE OF ORIGIN 1600s/1960s

FIRST USE Cattle herding

USE TODAY Companion

LIFE EXPECTANCY 12–13 years

OTHER NAME Ormskirk Heeler

WEIGHT RANGE
3–6 kg (6–13 lb)

HEIGHT RANGE
25–31 cm (10–12 in)

SWEDISH VALLHUND

Classified in Sweden as an indigenous breed, it is likely that this energetic herder descends from the bassets of continental Europe. Tenacious and tough, it is an ardent worker, and has the reckless courage typical of heelers. An excellent farm dog, it guards and drives livestock, protects property, and controls rodents. It makes a rewarding companion for seasoned dog handlers, but its instinct to nip never quite disappears. When kept in large numbers, Vallhunds are likely to fight among themselves.

Long neck has very muscular nape

Hard dense, medium-length coat, with fine, tight undercoat

KEY FACTS

COUNTRY OF ORIGIN Sweden

DATE OF ORIGIN Middle Ages

FIRST USE Cattle herding, guarding, ratting

USE TODAY Companion, herding, guarding, ratting

LIFE EXPECTANCY 12–14 years

OTHER NAMES Vallhund, Vasgötaspets, Swedish Cattle Dog

WEIGHT RANGE 11–15 kg (25–35 lb)

HEIGHT RANGE 31–35 cm (12–14 in)

GREY

RED-YELLOW

RED-BROWN

GREY-BROWN

BREED HISTORY In looks and temperament very similar to the Pembroke Welsh Corgi, it is likely that this multi-purpose drover, watchdog, and ratter arrived in Scandinavia with Vikings who had previously settled in Pembrokeshire, Wales. Its survival was ensured in the 1940s by a Swedish breeder, von Rosen.

Powerful legs, with short, oval feet, and round pads

AUSTRALIAN CATTLE DOG

In Great Britain, the now-extinct Blue Heeler was used at docks to herd sheep and cattle onto boats. Although its origins are radically different, the Australian Cattle Dog closely resembles the old dockyard breed. An Australian pioneer, Thomas Smith Hall, wanted a similar dog, but robust enough to withstand the hardships of driving cattle in 19th-century Australia. Exploiting the Dingo's ability to creep up silently on prey before biting, Hall created a dog very similar to today's Cattle Dog. The breed is wary by nature, and must be introduced to other animals and people when it is young.

KEY FACTS

COUNTRY OF ORIGIN Australia

DATE OF ORIGIN 1800s

FIRST USE Cattle herding

USE TODAY Cattle herding, companion

LIFE EXPECTANCY 12 years

OTHER NAMES Blue Heeler, Hall's Heeler, Queensland Heeler

WEIGHT RANGE
16–20 kg (35–45 lb)

HEIGHT RANGE
43–51 cm (17–20 in)

TAN

BLUE

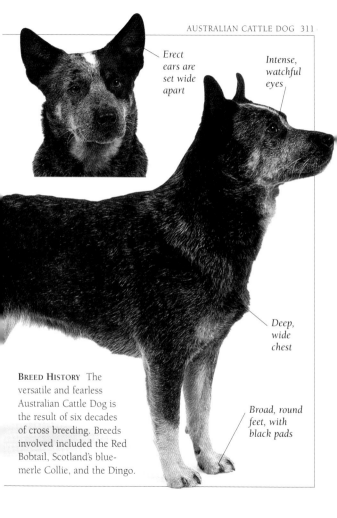

Erect ears are set wide apart

Intense, watchful eyes

Deep, wide chest

Broad, round feet, with black pads

BREED HISTORY The versatile and fearless Australian Cattle Dog is the result of six decades of cross breeding. Breeds involved included the Red Bobtail, Scotland's blue-merle Collie, and the Dingo.

AUSTRALIAN SHEPHERD DOG

Virtually unknown outside the United States, the Australian Shepherd is now increasing in popularity because of its obedient and willing nature, as well as its good looks. Originally bred as a working shepherd suitable for the varied climate of California, the Australian Shepherd has adapted superbly to both family life and work as a service dog, especially in search and rescue. It is affectionate and playful, but maintains a basic working instinct. This is not yet a "designer" dog, although reducing its size is an objective of some breeders.

KEY FACTS

COUNTRY OF ORIGIN United States/Australia/New Zealand

DATE OF ORIGIN 1900s

FIRST USE Sheep herding

USE TODAY Companion, sheep herding

LIFE EXPECTANCY 12–13 years

WEIGHT RANGE 16–32 kg (35–70 lb)

HEIGHT RANGE 46–58 cm (18–23 in)

Hind legs are well feathered with hair

BREED HISTORY This breed originated in California in the 1900s, although its ancestors include sheepdogs from New Zealand and Australia.

Predominantly brown nose

Body is moderately long

Moderately coarse topcoat

Thick ruff of fur on neck and chest

Solid, broad feet provide firm footing

RED

LIVER

BLACK

BLUE-MERLE

MAREMMA SHEEPDOG

This is a classic European flock-guarding dog, probably a close descendant of the great, white Eastern sheepdogs that slowly spread across Europe over 1,000 years ago. The Karabash and Akbash sheepdogs of Turkey, the Kuvac of Slovakia, the Kuvasz and Komondor of Hungary, and the Pyrenean Mountain Dog of France are all part of this migratory chain. The ancestors of the Maremma evolved to become smaller than their fellow herd guardians, while retaining the independence and aloofness of their heritage. Although it is now seen regularly in Great Britain, this breed is still rare in other countries outside Italy. It is strong willed and not easy to obedience train, but makes a superb guard.

V-shaped ears

KEY FACTS

COUNTRY OF ORIGIN Italy

DATE OF ORIGIN Antiquity

FIRST USE Flock guarding

USE TODAY Companion, security

LIFE EXPECTANCY 11–13 years

OTHER NAMES Maremma, Pastore Abruzzese, Cane da Pastore Maremmano-Abruzzese

WEIGHT RANGE
30–45 kg (66–100 lb)

HEIGHT RANGE
60–73 cm (23½–28½ in)

BREED HISTORY Today's Maremma Sheepdog is the descendant of the shorter-coated Maremmano Sheepdog and the longer-bodied Abruzzese Mountain Dog.

Deep, well-rounded rib cage extends to elbows

Very abundant, long, harsh hair has slight wave

Low-set tail is thickly feathered with dense hair

ANATOLIAN (KARABASH) DOG

Turkish shepherds never used dogs to herd sheep, only to protect them from predators. These sheepdogs were collectively classified as "coban kopegi", but in the 1970s breeders began to investigate regional variations. Karabash-type sheepdogs are found in central Turkey, and closely resemble the sheepdogs of eastern Turkey. In its native land, the Karabash remains a guardian, protecting flocks from wolves, bears, and jackals. Strong willed and independent, it is not an entirely suitable companion, although with careful socialization it can adapt fairly well to a family environment.

KEY FACTS

COUNTRY OF ORIGIN Turkey

DATE OF ORIGIN Middle Ages

FIRST USE Sheep guarding

USE TODAY Sheep guarding

LIFE EXPECTANCY 10–11 years

OTHER NAMES Coban Kopegi, Karabas, Kangal Dog, Anatolian Shepherd Dog

WEIGHT RANGE 41–64 kg (90–141 lb)

HEIGHT RANGE 71–81 cm (28–32 in)

Flat coat is short and dense, with thick undercoat

VARIETY
OF
COLOURS

*Triangular ears
are carried high
when dog is alert*

*Thick, powerful,
muscular neck*

*Long, straight
forelegs are wide set*

*Short nails
on strong
feet, with
well-arched
toes*

BREED HISTORY About 1,000
years ago, the Turkic-speaking
people entered Asia Minor,
occupying the region that is
now Turkey. They brought with
them their great, herd-guarding
dogs. The Karabash descends
from these dogs.

KOMONDOR

The Komondor's corded coat historically provided protection from both the elements and from wolves, as the breed guarded sheep and cattle in Hungary over the centuries. Its strong guarding ability is used today to protect sheep in North America from coyote predation. The dog is raised from puppyhood with its flock of sheep, and is shorn when the sheep are shorn. It makes an amenable companion, although its coat requires constant attention to prevent the cords from becoming matted.

KEY FACTS

COUNTRY OF ORIGIN Hungary

DATE OF ORIGIN Antiquity

FIRST USE Sheep guarding

USE TODAY Livestock guarding, companion

LIFE EXPECTANCY 12 years

OTHER NAME Hungarian Sheepdog

WEIGHT RANGE
36–61 kg (80–135 lb)

HEIGHT RANGE
65–90 cm (26½–35½ in)

Strong, heavy cords feel like felt when touched

BREED HISTORY It is thought that this, the largest of the Hungarian herdsmen's dogs, accompanied the Magyar tribe from the east when it settled in Hungary over 1,000 years ago. Although first mentioned by name in 1544, it was not until around 1910 that the Komondor was firmly established as a modern breed.

Muscular neck, with grey-pigmented skin under hair

Heavy, coarse topcoat, with dense, woolly, soft undercoat

HUNGARIAN KUVASZ

Although Hungarian history books say that in the 15th century King Matthias I used the Kuvasz to hunt wild boars, this breed is not a natural hunter. It is an inveterate guard, content to stay with its flock rather than to participate in a hunt. The Kuvasz is a powerful dog that willingly defends its territory, and is best in the hands of capable dog handlers. However, it does make a loyal companion and is usually reliable with its human family.

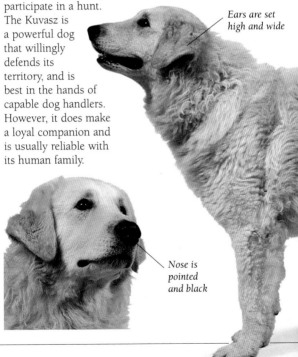

Ears are set high and wide

Nose is pointed and black

BREED HISTORY Some authorities believe that this great, white guard dog arrived in Hungary in the 1100s with the Kumans – nomadic Turkish shepherds. First mentioned as a breed in the 1600s, the Kuvasz's name comes from the Turkish *kavas* or *kawasz*, meaning armed guard, which it certainly is.

KEY FACTS

COUNTRY OF ORIGIN Hungary

DATE OF ORIGIN Middle Ages

FIRST USE Livestock guarding

USE TODAY Companion, security

LIFE EXPECTANCY 12–14 years

OTHER NAME Kuvasz

WEIGHT RANGE
30–52 kg (66–115 lb)

HEIGHT RANGE
66–75 cm (26–29½ in)

Coat is rough, wavy, and stiff

Thighs and hind legs are very muscular

Hind feet are longer than front feet, but just as strong

POLISH LOWLAND SHEEPDOG

Breed aficionados consider the Polish Lowland Sheepdog to be an important link between ancient, corded Asian herding dogs, brought to Europe over 1,000 years ago, and more recent, shaggy herders, such as the Scottish Bearded Collie and Dutch Schapendoes. This breed was revived by diligent Polish breeders after World War II. Popular in Poland and elsewhere, it is generally kept as a household companion, although it remains an excellent herder.

Long, dense, shaggy coat covers entire body

KEY FACTS

COUNTRY OF ORIGIN Poland

DATE OF ORIGIN 1500s

FIRST USE Hunting

USE TODAY Companion, herding

LIFE EXPECTANCY 13–14 years

OTHER NAME Polski Owczarek Nizinny

WEIGHT RANGE
14–16 kg (30–35 lb)

HEIGHT RANGE
41–51 cm (16–20 in)

BREED HISTORY It is likely that this medium-sized, robust sheepdog evolved from ancient, corded herding dogs from the Hungarian plains, which were bred with other small, long-coated mountain herders. The ravages of World War II very nearly led to the breed's extinction.

Copious hair on forehead, cheeks, and chin

Back is level and fairly broad

Ribs are moderately well sprung

Legs are covered with dense, harsh hair

ANY COLOUR

BRIARD

American soldiers introduced this ruggedly muscular breed to the United States after World War I, but it took 50 years to gain a solid foothold. Today, this is one of France's most popular companion dogs, although it was only in the 1970s that breeders addressed the problem of shyness and nervous aggression in the breed. With careful selection, it is well mannered with its human family, yet retains superb guarding instincts. It is also an excellent herding dog, well insulated by its thick coat against harsh weather conditions.

BREED HISTORY The Briard's ancient origins are unknown, but it was once classified as the goat-haired variety of the Beauceron. It has been suggested that it was developed by crossing that breed with the French Barbet (a possible forerunner of the poodle). Named after the province of Brie, the watchful Briard has been a shepherd's guardian throughout France.

KEY FACTS

COUNTRY OF ORIGIN France

DATE OF ORIGIN Middle Ages/1800s

FIRST USE Livestock guarding/herding

USE TODAY Companion, security

LIFE EXPECTANCY 11–13 years

OTHER NAME Berger de Brie

WEIGHT RANGE
33.5–34.5 kg (74–76 lb)

HEIGHT RANGE
57–69 cm (23–27 in)

FAWN

BLACK

Large, calm-looking eyes

Muzzle is square, with black nose

High-set, short ears covered with hair

Prominent, distinctive beard

Long, flexible, dry hair, like that of a goat

Broad, deep chest

BEAUCERON

This strong-willed, active breed needs firm handling and a great deal of exercise – in return it gives lifelong companionship and protection. Physically uncomplicated, it has an agile, smoothly powerful body. Obedience training can sometimes be difficult, and first meetings with other adult dogs should be carried out under supervision. However, like the Briard, the Beauceron is almost invariably a safe and responsible member of its own family. A reliable working dog, it is also becoming increasingly popular in European show rings.

Rough, short, dense, close-fitting coat

Double dewclaws on hind feet

KEY FACTS

COUNTRY OF ORIGIN France

DATE OF ORIGIN Middle Ages

FIRST USE Boar herding/ guarding/hunting

USE TODAY Companion

LIFE EXPECTANCY 11–13 years

OTHER NAMES Berger de Beauce, Bas Rouge, Beauce Shepherd

WEIGHT RANGE
30–39 kg (66–85 lb)

HEIGHT RANGE
64–71 cm (25–28 in)

Eyes vary in colour, according to coat

Long head, with flat, but slightly domed, skull

BREED HISTORY

Originally from the French province of Brie, the Beauceron is closely related to the Briard – each has a double dewclaw (the fifth digit on the hind feet). In looks a cross between the Mastiff and the Dobermann, this breed's anatomy is strikingly similar to 2,000-year-old skeletal remains found in eastern France.

BLACK/ TAN

BLACK

HARLEQUIN

Long, straight forelegs, with round feet and black nails

BOUVIER DES FLANDRES

This robust, cattle-driving, cart-pulling farm dog existed in a number of coat and colour varieties until 1965, when present standards were written. During World War I, the French army used the Bouvier in its medical corps, but numbers declined drastically shortly afterwards. It was only through the intervention of the Belgian Kennel Club that the breed was rescued from oblivion. This powerful and usually amiable dog can be quite aggressive (a reminder of its cattle-guarding heritage), and it makes a superb guard dog. Popular in its native land, it is also highly regarded in North America, both as a companion and as a farm worker.

VARIETY
OF
COLOURS

Short, round, compact feet

High-set ears are quite small in proportion to large head

Back is short, broad, and powerful

Topcoat is dry, dull, and crisp to the touch

Fluffy, fine undercoat

KEY FACTS

COUNTRY OF ORIGIN Belgium/France

DATE OF ORIGIN 1600s

FIRST USE Cattle herding

USE TODAY Companion, guarding

LIFE EXPECTANCY 11–12 years

WEIGHT RANGE
27–40 kg (60–88 lb)

HEIGHT RANGE
58–69 cm (23–27 in)

BREED HISTORY With the exception of the nearly extinct Bouvier des Ardennes, this breed is the sole survivor of the once wide variety of Belgian bouviers, or cattle dogs. It may have developed from griffons (rough-coated scent hounds) and the old-type Beauceron.

BERGAMASCO

In looks and temperament, this hardy and adaptable breed is remarkably similar to the Briard. However, while the Briard is popular both in France and abroad, the Bergamasco is relatively unknown, both inside and outside its native land, and has often been close to extinction. An exceptionally efficient worker, its distinctive corded coat evolved to protect it both from the weather and from the flailing hooves of livestock. Affectionate, courageous, and loyal, the Bergamasco makes a superb companion and guard dog, although it is not well suited to life in the city.

No "flocking" of hair on puppy's coat

Hare-like feet, with lean pads and black nails

KEY FACTS

COUNTRY OF ORIGIN Italy

DATE OF ORIGIN Antiquity

FIRST USE Livestock guarding

USE TODAY Companion, guarding

LIFE EXPECTANCY 11–13 years

OTHER NAMES Bergamese Shepherd, Cane da Pastore Bergamasco

WEIGHT RANGE
26–38 kg (57–84 lb)

HEIGHT RANGE
56–61 cm (22–24 in)

BREED HISTORY Two thousand
years ago, Roman writers on
agriculture described the ideal
sheepdog – not as swift as the
hound or as strong as the yard
dog, but agile and fearless
enough to repel wolves and
follow in pursuit. Today's
Bergamasco, named after
the Bergamo region of
northern Italy, follows
that requirement.

*Fine-textured
facial hair covers
tapering muzzle*

*Soft, long hair
forms strong,
wavy cords,
or "flocks"*

PORTUGUESE SHEPHERD DOG

For most of the 20th century, the Portuguese Shepherd Dog was the companion of poor shepherds in southern Portugal, but by the 1970s it was almost extinct. Fortunately, the beauty of its coat and its pliant disposition came to the notice of breeders, and today its appeal to middle-class Portuguese dog owners ensures its survival. An excellent breed, it is very easy to obedience train, good with children and with other dogs, and unlikely to snap or bite unless provoked. Although it is virtually unknown outside its native land, this unkempt-looking canine is a classic dog, worthy of more international acclaim.

KEY FACTS

COUNTRY OF ORIGIN Portugal

DATE OF ORIGIN 1800s

FIRST USE Livestock herding

USE TODAY Companion, herding

LIFE EXPECTANCY 12–13 years

OTHER NAME Cão da Serra de Aires

WEIGHT RANGE
12–18 kg (26–40 lb)

HEIGHT RANGE
41–56 cm (16–22 in)

YELLOW

FAWN

GREY

BROWN

BLACK

BREED HISTORY This shaggy, all-purpose herder, drover, and guardian dog from the southern plains of Portugal may descend from Briards imported by Count de Castro Guimaraes, which then bred with local mountain dogs, or perhaps the Catalan Sheepdog from Catalonia, in Spain.

Moderate-sized ears hang down sides of cheeks

Dark eyes

Long fur covers forelimbs

ESTRELA MOUNTAIN DOG

For centuries, this mastiff has herded and defended flocks from wolves, while accompanying shepherds in the Estrela mountains of Portugal. The dense, double coat, particularly of the long-haired variety, provides protection in cold weather. Although it still serves these functions, today this calm, but naturally dominant, dog is also kept as a companion. Outside Portugal, it has received most recognition in Great Britain, where it is often seen at dog shows. Although hip dysplasia can be a problem, this is generally a healthy breed, but one that needs firm handling.

KEY FACTS

COUNTRY OF ORIGIN Portugal

DATE OF ORIGIN Middle Ages

FIRST USE Livestock guarding

USE TODAY Companion, livestock dog

LIFE EXPECTANCY 11–13 years

OTHER NAMES Cão da Serra da Estrela, Portuguese Sheepdog

WEIGHT RANGE
30–50 kg (66–110 lb)

HEIGHT RANGE
62–72 cm (24½–28½ in)

BREED HISTORY This most popular of all Portuguese breeds is one of the oldest on the Iberian peninsula. It is descended from ancient Asiatic mastiffs brought to the West, and is related to the Spanish Mastiff. Having suffered from unorthodox cross breeding with the German Shepherd in the 1900s, it is now back to a pure form.

Oval, medium-sized eyes are set horizontally

Abundant topcoat is darker than equally thick undercoat

Thick forelimbs are well boned

FAWN

RED BRINDLE

BLACK BRINDLE

PYRENEAN MOUNTAIN DOG

The first Pyreneans to be kept as pets had rather assertive, warrior-like personalities. In recent years, breeders have been very successful in diminishing this characteristic, while at the same time retaining other, attractive qualities, such as patience, nobility, and courage. This dog will, however, still go into a defence mode if its territory is invaded. Today the breed is firmly established in Great Britain, North America, and France. Its great size makes it unsuitable for urban environments, unless there is open space nearby.

KEY FACTS

COUNTRY OF ORIGIN France

DATE OF ORIGIN Antiquity

FIRST USE Sheep guarding

USE TODAY Companion, guarding

LIFE EXPECTANCY 11–12 years

OTHER NAMES Great Pyrenees, Chien de Montagne des Pyrénées

WEIGHT RANGE
45–60 kg (99–132 lb)

HEIGHT RANGE
65–81 cm (26–32 in)

Paws are rather small and compact

Small, triangular ears are set at eye level, hanging against head

Small, amber eyes have serene expression

BREED HISTORY One of the great, white guarding mastiffs that spread across Europe, this magnificent breed is probably related to the Italian Maremma, Hungarian Kuvasz, and Turkish Karabash.

Hair on forelimbs forms a woolly fringe

PYRENEAN SHEEPDOG

This is a lively breed, built for speed, endurance, and an active life. Its three different coat types are the strongest indication that it has been bred to work in specific climates, not to meet show specifications. In its mountainous home, it once worked in tandem with the Pyrenean Mountain Dog, herding and driving sheep, while the Mountain Dog guarded the flock from mountain wolves. The coat of the long-haired variety gives excellent weatherproofing, even in harsh winters. The breed's relatively small size and trainability make it a good household companion.

KEY FACTS

COUNTRY OF ORIGIN France

DATE OF ORIGIN 1700s

FIRST USE Sheep herding/guarding

USE TODAY Companion, herding, guarding

LIFE EXPECTANCY 12 years

OTHER NAMES Labrit, Berger des Pyrénées

WEIGHT RANGE
8–15 kg (18–33 lb)

HEIGHT RANGE
38–56 cm (15–22 in)

BREED HISTORY A slight, small relative of the Catalan Sheepdog from Spain, the Pyrenean exists in long-haired, goat-haired, and smooth-haired forms. An agile, durable breed, it evolved in the French Pyrenean district between Lourdes and Gavarnie, to suit the needs of mountain shepherds.

Black-rimmed, expressive, dark-brown eyes

Long hair on head and cheeks

Coat is short and fine on face

FAWN

GREY

RED BRINDLE

BLUE

BLACK BRINDLE

BERNESE MOUNTAIN DOG

The popularity of the Bernese is rapidly increasing in both Europe and North America. In the 1930s, a number of breeders bred for increased size and guarding ability, which left a trait of temperamental unreliability in certain lines, leading to a tendency towards unprovoked aggression. Also, breeding from a small genetic stock has created certain problems, particularly shoulder lameness. A working breed, trained to herd livestock and pull carts, the Bernese readily learns obedience, and is successful in the show ring. It can be a sloppily affectionate giant, but it is best in the hands of an experienced dog handler.

Fluffy tail does not curl

KEY FACTS

COUNTRY OF ORIGIN Switzerland

DATE OF ORIGIN Antiquity/1900s

FIRST USE Draughting

USE TODAY Companion

LIFE EXPECTANCY 10–12 years

OTHER NAME Berner Sennenhund, Bernese Cattle Dog

WEIGHT RANGE
40–44 kg (87–90 lb)

HEIGHT RANGE
58–70 cm (23–27½ in)

BREED HISTORY Another ancient breed, the Bernese had almost disappeared in the late 1800s when Franz Schertenlieb, a breeder investigating the history of Swiss mountain dogs, found several good individuals in the Berne region. This breed was given its present name in 1908.

Long muzzle, with medium-sized nose

Glossy, black coat is abundant, long, and smooth

Forelimbs are robust

White hair on chest also occurs on bridge of nose and feet

GREAT SWISS MOUNTAIN DOG

With the exception of the St. Bernard, this breed is the largest of the Swiss mountain dogs, and may also be the oldest. For centuries, it was a popular draught dog in villages and on farms. Its numbers were bolstered in the early 1900s through the work of Franz Schertenlieb and Albert Heim, who located enough dogs to revitalize the breed. The Great Swiss Mountain Dog is gentle with humans, but can sometimes be troublesome with other dogs.

KEY FACTS

COUNTRY OF ORIGIN Switzerland

DATE OF ORIGIN Antiquity/1900s

FIRST USE Draughting

USE TODAY Companion

LIFE EXPECTANCY 10–11 years

OTHER NAMES Grosser Schweizer Sennenhund, Great Swiss Cattle Dog

WEIGHT RANGE
59–61 kg (130–135 lb)

HEIGHT RANGE
60–72 cm (23½–28½ in)

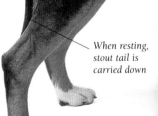

When resting, stout tail is carried down

Robust head, with slight furrow down muzzle

Well-fitted, close eyelids

Hard topcoat covers full undercoat

Fold of skin by larynx

Short, round feet, with arched toes

BREED HISTORY Another probable descendant of the great Roman mastiffs, this breed was "discovered" in the early 1900s by Franz Schertenlieb. He took his discovery to Albert Heim, who had thought the dog extinct. Revitalized through their efforts, the breed achieved recognition under its present name in 1910.

St. Bernard

Whether the St. Bernard ever actually rescued snowbound alpine travellers is debatable, but that image is irreversibly established. The Bernardine Hospice has kept this kindly breed since the 1660s – Bernardine monks used it for draught work, and boasted of its hauling abilities. It was also used to make trails through fresh snow. Today's benevolent hulk is an impressively muscular giant, whose mammoth size makes it unsuitable for most forms of indoor living.

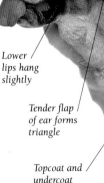

Lower lips hang slightly

Tender flap of ear forms triangle

Topcoat and undercoat are dense

Key Facts

Country of origin Switzerland

Date of origin Middle Ages

First use Hauling, companion

Use today Companion

Life expectancy 11 years

Other name Alpine Mastiff

Weight range
50–91 kg (110–200 lb)

Height range
61–71 cm (24–28 in)

BREED HISTORY Descended from alpine mastiffs first brought to Switzerland with the passing Roman army, the St. Bernard was once an aggressive, short-coated breed. At one time it was virtually extinct, but it was revitalized, possibly using Newfoundland and Great Dane bloodlines. The breed's name came into general use in 1865.

Friendly eyes set to front

Broad, powerful tail curls slightly at tip

ORANGE

RED BRINDLE

BROWN BRINDLE

LEONBERGER

This genial giant almost became extinct during World War II, but in the last 20 years has gained a good foothold, both in its home country, and in Great Britain and North America. When the Leonberger was first exhibited, it was dismissed as a mere cross of several breeds, which is exactly what it is. However, the breed is a strikingly handsome dog. An inveterate swimmer, the Leonberger is willing to dog paddle in the coldest weather. Its great size makes it rather unsuitable for urban living. As with many breeds that have been "recreated", hip dysplasia can be a concern to some breeders.

Large, round feet, with webbed toes, aid swimming

KEY FACTS

COUNTRY OF ORIGIN Germany

DATE OF ORIGIN 1800s

FIRST USE Companion

USE TODAY Companion

LIFE EXPECTANCY 11 years

WEIGHT RANGE
34–50 kg (75–110 lb)

HEIGHT RANGE
65–80 cm (26–31½ in)

YELLOW, GOLD

RED-BROWN

Brown eyes have friendly expression

Ears are as wide as they are long

Smooth, dense coat has slight wave, but does not obscure body shape

BREED HISTORY

This distinguished breed was produced to resemble the lion on the coat of arms of the town hall of Leonberg, Germany. It was developed using the Newfoundland, Landseer (classified as a Newfoundland colour variety in North America and Great Britain), St. Bernard, and Pyrenean Mountain Dog.

Forelegs are fairly wide set, with well-articulated joints

NEWFOUNDLAND

One of the friendliest of all breeds, the Newfoundland was originally used in cod fisheries to pull nets ashore, and to pull boats. Today, teams of Newfoundlands are used in France to assist the emergency services in sea rescue. Land-based tests include draught work and negotiating an obstacle course. If this benign, happy breed has a behavioural drawback, it is its inclination to rescue anyone from the water, regardless of their desire or need to be rescued. Although a little prone to drooling saliva, it is a benevolent giant and a loyal friend.

Topcoat is flat, dense, somewhat coarse, and oily

Fairly thick tail is well covered in hair

Feet are large and well shaped, with broadly webbed toes

BROWN

BLACK

Small, dark eyes

Broad and massive head, with short, square, clean-cut muzzle

BREED HISTORY
Descended from the now-extinct Greater St. John's Dog, this large, water-loving breed has been bred to its present standard for over 100 years. Native North American, Viking, and Iberian breeds may be included in the dog's background.

KEY FACTS

COUNTRY OF ORIGIN Canada
DATE OF ORIGIN 1700s
FIRST USE Helping fishermen
USE TODAY Companion, rescue
LIFE EXPECTANCY 11 years
WEIGHT RANGE
50–68 kg (110–150 lb)
HEIGHT RANGE
66–71 cm (26–28 in)

HOVAWART

The Hovawart is a classic example of the diligence of German dog breeding 100 years ago. In an attempt to recreate the great estate-guarding dog of the Middle Ages, a group of dedicated breeders used selected farm dogs acquired in the Black Forest and Hartz mountain regions of Germany, and perhaps the Hungarian Kuvasz, German Shepherd, and Newfoundland, to produce this elegant worker, first recognized in 1936. The Hovawart is a reserved but pleasant family dog, although some strains are prone to fear biting, and others may be rather timid. The breed is, however, easy to obedience train and gets on well with other dogs and children.

Straight, strong, well-fringed forelegs, with moderate-sized feet

BREED HISTORY The "Hofwarth", an estate guard dog, is first mentioned in 1220, in Eike von Repgow's *Sachsenspiegel*. Records from the 1400s illustrate and describe this breed tracking robbers. Today's Hovawart is a 20th-century recreation of this ancient guarding dog.

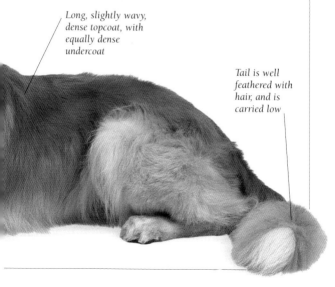

Long, slightly wavy, dense topcoat, with equally dense undercoat

Tail is well feathered with hair, and is carried low

ROTTWEILER

Powerful in body and jaws, the Rottweiler can offer formidable protection. Today, this impressively handsome dog, the descendant of ancient boar hunters, is popular throughout the world, as both a family dog and a guard dog. Easy to obedience train, it can show its temper; breeders, notably in Scandinavia, have reduced this trait.

KEY FACTS

COUNTRY OF ORIGIN Germany

DATE OF ORIGIN 1820s

FIRST USE Cattle/guard dog

USE TODAY Companion, police dog, guarding

LIFE EXPECTANCY 11–12 years

WEIGHT RANGE
41–50 kg (90–110 lb)

HEIGHT RANGE
58–69 cm (23–27 in)

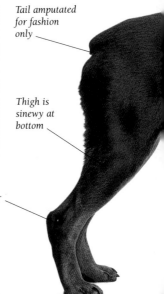

Tail amputated for fashion only

Thigh is sinewy at bottom

Hind legs longer than front legs

BREED HISTORY The Rottweiler was bred in Rottweil, southern Germany, in the 1800s, as a distinct drover and guard dog.

High, wide-set ears are proportionately rather small

Slightly arched neck is strong, round, and very muscular

Topcoat is coarse and flat

Legs have plenty of thick bone

DOBERMANN

The elegant, often affectionate Dobermann is a classic example of the industriously successful dog-breeding programmes that took place in Germany just over 100 years ago. Today, this obedient, alert, and resourceful breed is a companion and service dog all over the world. Due to unscrupulous breeding, nervousness and fear biting can occur in some individuals. Good breeders, however, ensure that their dogs are neither shy nor vicious, and that they are well socialized before going to a new home. Heart disease is, unfortunately, becoming an increasingly serious problem for the breed.

Thick hair is smooth, glossy, and hard

KEY FACTS

COUNTRY OF ORIGIN Germany

DATE OF ORIGIN 1800s

FIRST USE Guarding

USE TODAY Companion, security

LIFE EXPECTANCY 12 years

OTHER NAME Doberman Pinscher

WEIGHT RANGE
30–40 kg (66–88 lb)

HEIGHT RANGE
65–69 cm (25½–27 in)

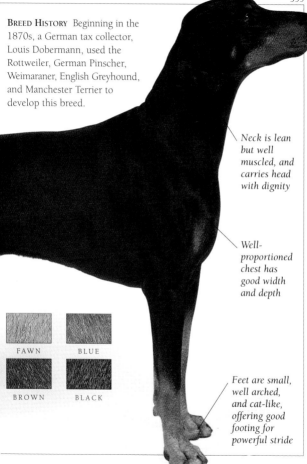

BREED HISTORY Beginning in the 1870s, a German tax collector, Louis Dobermann, used the Rottweiler, German Pinscher, Weimaraner, English Greyhound, and Manchester Terrier to develop this breed.

Neck is lean but well muscled, and carries head with dignity

Well-proportioned chest has good width and depth

FAWN

BLUE

BROWN

BLACK

Feet are small, well arched, and cat-like, offering good footing for powerful stride

SCHNAUZER

A vigilant guard, this is the original breed from which miniature and giant breeds later evolved. The German artist Albrecht Dürer painted dogs of this conformation, as did Rembrandt. It is possible that this ancient breed is a cross between spitz and guarding dogs. Although today it is kept primarily as a companion, the Schnauzer remains an excellent livestock dog. It learns obedience reasonably easily, and can be trained to retrieve both on land and from water.

KEY FACTS

COUNTRY OF ORIGIN Germany

DATE OF ORIGIN Middle Ages

FIRST USE Ratting, guarding

USE TODAY Companion

LIFE EXPECTANCY 12–14 years

OTHER NAME Mittelschnauzer

WEIGHT RANGE
14.5–15.5 kg (32–34 lb)

HEIGHT RANGE
45–50 cm (18–20 in)

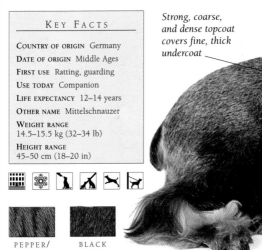

Strong, coarse, and dense topcoat covers fine, thick undercoat

PEPPER/
SALT

BLACK

BREED HISTORY Once a ratter as well as a guard, the Schnauzer is often classified as a terrier. The breed originated in southern Germany and adjacent regions of Switzerland and France, and was once known as the Schnauzer-Pinscher.

Long, powerful head gradually narrows from ears to tip of nose

Ears are partly erect, dropping gracefully to sides

Long muzzle and chin hair give distinctive and amusing appearance

Area between chest and forelegs is broad

GIANT SCHNAUZER

At one time, the Giant Schnauzer was a common herding breed in southern Germany, but its extensive feeding requirements in hard times reduced its appeal. In the latter part of the 19th century, the dog regained popularity as a butcher's drover and guard. Although hardy and vigorous, it has a tendency towards both shoulder and hip arthritis. The Giant Schnauzer does not demand unlimited exercise, making it suitable for city life. However, this breed is not afraid to use its considerable power to defend its territory.

Robust and powerful front legs are not set too close together

PEPPER/
SALT

BLACK

KEY FACTS

COUNTRY OF ORIGIN Germany

DATE OF ORIGIN Middle Ages

FIRST USE Cattle herding

USE TODAY Companion, service

LIFE EXPECTANCY 11–12 years

OTHER NAME Riesenschnauzer

WEIGHT RANGE
32–35 kg (70–77 lb)

HEIGHT RANGE
59–70 cm (23½–27½ in)

*Beard is long
and coarse*

*From chest to
forelegs, body is
long and wide*

*Thighs are
strong and
well muscled*

BREED HISTORY

The most powerful
of the German
schnauzers, this
reliable dog was
developed by
increasing the size
of the standard
Schnauzer. When
the breed was
first exhibited in
Munich, Germany,
in 1909, it was
called the Russian
Bear Schnauzer.

MASTIFF

Throughout its long history, the Mastiff has contributed to the development of a variety of dog breeds, including the Bullmastiff. The name probably evolved from the Anglo-Saxon word *masty*, meaning powerful. The Mastiff is now a rare sight. One of the largest dogs in the world, it is exceptionally powerful, and requires ample space to live in and plenty of food. It is generally easygoing, but can be very protective of its owners and must be handled sensibly.

KEY FACTS

COUNTRY OF ORIGIN Great Britain

DATE OF ORIGIN Antiquity

FIRST USE Guarding

USE TODAY Companion, guarding

LIFE EXPECTANCY 10–12 years

OTHER NAME English Mastiff

WEIGHT RANGE
79–86 kg (175–190 lb)

HEIGHT RANGE
70–76 cm (27½–30 in)

Forelegs are straight, densely boned, and set firmly apart

Large, round feet, with well-arched toes and black nails

BREED HISTORY The Mastiff existed in Great Britain 2,000 years ago, and was exported to Rome as a military and fighting dog. It may have arrived from Asia via Mediterranean and Phoenician traders, or with other traders across the Urals and northern Europe.

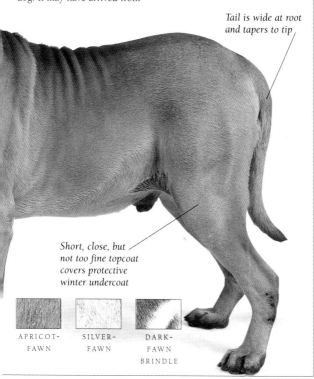

Tail is wide at root and tapers to tip

Short, close, but not too fine topcoat covers protective winter undercoat

APRICOT-FAWN

SILVER-FAWN

DARK-FAWN BRINDLE

FRENCH MASTIFF

More similar to the recently developed Bullmastiff than to the ancient English Mastiff, this very old breed was originally used for boar and bear hunting in southern France, and then for cattle driving. Because of its fearlessness, the French Mastiff was also used in the animal-baiting arena and the dog-fight ring. It was not until the breed appeared in an American film in 1989 with Tom Hanks that it attained any recognition outside France. Unlike the sloppy star of *Turner and Hooch*, the French Mastiff possesses formidable traits, such as relentless strength, wariness of strangers, and an inclination to intimidate unknown people.

No feathering of hair on deeply set, thick tail

KEY FACTS

COUNTRY OF ORIGIN France

DATE OF ORIGIN Antiquity

FIRST USE Guarding, game hunting

USE TODAY Companion, guarding

LIFE EXPECTANCY 10–12 years

OTHER NAME Dogue de Bordeaux

WEIGHT RANGE
36–45 kg (80–100 lb)

HEIGHT RANGE
58–69 cm (23–27 in)

BREED HISTORY For centuries, the Bordeaux region of France was ruled by English kings. The large guard dogs in that area were almost certainly crossed with the English Mastiff, together with similar dogs from Spain, resulting in this powerful, and at one time ferocious, mastiff.

GOLDEN, FAWN

MAHOGANY

Wide-set, oval eyes have prominent upper ridges

Huge head, furrowed with wrinkles, gives pugnacious appearance

NEAPOLITAN MASTIFF

The Roman writer Columella's description of the perfect house guard could apply to this ponderous breed, which was saved from oblivion less than 50 years ago. A superb drooler, the Neapolitan Mastiff needs early socialization and obedience training, and males can be dominant. It does not demand frequent exercise, but its messy eating manners and sheer size make it difficult to keep inside a home. This breed is best in the hands of experienced dog handlers.

Ears are surgically removed solely to follow fashion

KEY FACTS

COUNTRY OF ORIGIN Italy

DATE OF ORIGIN Antiquity

FIRST USE Livestock guarding, dog fighting

USE TODAY Companion, security

LIFE EXPECTANCY 10–11 years

OTHER NAME Mastino Napoletano

WEIGHT RANGE
50–68 kg (110–150 lb)

HEIGHT RANGE
65–75 cm (26–29 in)

GREY

BROWN

RED BRINDLE

BLACK BRINDLE

BLUE

BLACK

BREED HISTORY Present in the central Italian region of Campania since ancient times, but not exhibited until 1947, the Neapolitan Mastiff probably descends from Roman fighting, war, and circus mastiffs. These dogs reached Rome via Greece, transported there from Asia by Alexander the Great.

Heavy upper lips

Dense, fine, short, smooth hair

Very well-developed muscles cover deep chest

Thigh muscles are long and broad

TIBETAN MASTIFF

The Tibetan Mastiff once protected livestock in the Himalayas and Tibet, and is now a European-bred show dog, still uncommon but established throughout Europe. Large boned and big headed, this massive dog has provided the root stock for the mountain, livestock, and fighting dogs of Europe, the Americas, and even Japan. Easygoing and affably aloof, it is content to be one of life's observers, although it will not hesitate to defend what it feels to be its territory.

BREED HISTORY Rescued from extinction by British breeders in the 1800s, the Tibetan Mastiff is the parent breed of most European mastiffs. Originally used to flock herds and to guard the home, the Tibetan Mastiff was prized for both its courage and its impressive size.

Huge, broad head, with smooth face

KEY FACTS

COUNTRY OF ORIGIN Tibet

DATE OF ORIGIN Antiquity

FIRST USE Livestock guarding

USE TODAY Companion, guarding

LIFE EXPECTANCY 11 years

OTHER NAME Do-Khyi

WEIGHT RANGE
64–82 kg (140–180 lb)

HEIGHT RANGE
61–71 cm (24–28 in)

GREY

GOLD

BLACK

BROWN

BLACK/
TAN

Solidly boned legs

Long, straight coat, with thick and heavy undercoat

BULLDOG

Few breeds have altered as radically in form, function, and personality as the Bulldog. The word "bulldog" was in use in the 1600s, to denote the breed that was a cross between mastiff guard dogs used in bear baiting, and tenacious terriers used in game hunting. Strong and resolute, the Bulldog was an ideal pit dog, ruthlessly hanging onto the bull, regardless of the injuries it suffered. Today's gentle dog has been constructed solely for the show ring, which has caused a number of health problems. This is a great pity, since the breed has a delightful personality and makes an engaging companion.

KEY FACTS

COUNTRY OF ORIGIN Great Britain

DATE OF ORIGIN 1800s

FIRST USE Bull baiting

USE TODAY Companion

LIFE EXPECTANCY 9–11 years

OTHER NAME English Bulldog

WEIGHT RANGE
23–25 kg (50–55 lb)

HEIGHT RANGE
31–36 cm (12–14 in)

BREED HISTORY
When the "sport" of bull baiting became illegal in Great Britain in the 1830s, this ferociously tenacious breed was in danger of extinction. Bill George, a breeder, successfully transformed the Bulldog into its present form, reducing its aggressive nature.

Eyes and nose are
very close together

Lips
hang
over
lower
jaws

Solid, muscular
forelegs are set
very wide apart

Thickly skinned
feet turn out
slightly

VARIETY
OF
COLOURS

BULLMASTIFF

In theory, the Bullmastiff should be one of the world's most popular guard dogs. Its endurance, strength, and speed were developed so that it could overtake and capture intruders without mauling or killing them. Handsome and powerful, it has spread throughout all the continents of the world, but has never attained the popularity of its German equivalent, the Rottweiler. The reason for this is that the Bullmastiff can be a stubborn breed, resistant to obedience training, and overly protective of its human family.

KEY FACTS

COUNTRY OF ORIGIN Great Britain

DATE OF ORIGIN 1800s

FIRST USE Guarding

USE TODAY Companion, guarding

LIFE EXPECTANCY 10–12 years

WEIGHT RANGE
41–59 kg (90–130 lb)

HEIGHT RANGE
64–69 cm (25–27 in)

Muscular, thick neck blends into chest

Powerful forelegs are thick and straight

Large, but compact, cat-like feet, with rounded toes

BREED HISTORY The foundation stock of this formidable breed is 60 per cent English Mastiff and 40 per cent Bulldog. The Bullmastiff was produced to act as a gamekeeper's assistant, with the ability to chase and immobilize poachers on estates.

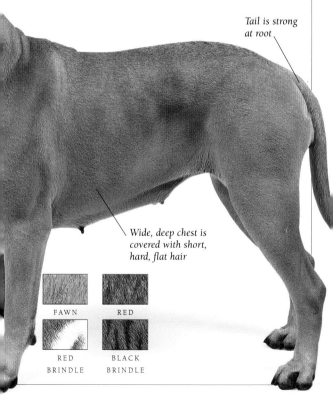

Tail is strong at root

Wide, deep chest is covered with short, hard, flat hair

FAWN

RED

RED BRINDLE

BLACK BRINDLE

BOXER

The boisterous and self-confident Boxer is one of the great successes of the high-quality "designer" dog breeding that took place in Germany 100 years ago. Today, although the Boxer's size varies from country to country, its personality remains the same – active, positive, strong, and fun loving. The Boxer is in many ways an ideal family dog, but due to its lifelong puppy-like behaviour, fast reaction time, and relatively large size, it can create unintentional havoc. The breed's muscular and intimidating appearance makes it an excellent house protector; at the same time, it is as gentle as a lamb with children.

Short, shiny, smooth hair covers impressive chest reaching down to elbows

Large, compact feet, with strong toes

FAWN

BLACK
BRINDLE

KEY FACTS

COUNTRY OF ORIGIN Germany

DATE OF ORIGIN 1850s

FIRST USE Guarding, bull baiting

USE TODAY Companion

LIFE EXPECTANCY 12 years

WEIGHT RANGE
25–32 kg (55–70 lb)

HEIGHT RANGE
53–63 cm (21–25 in)

*Well-muscled,
powerful loins
allow for freedom
of movement and
an elegant stride*

*Long thighs
are broad,
curved, and
very powerful*

BREED HISTORY
The Boxer's primary
ancestor, the old
Bullenbeisser, was
used in Germany
and the Netherlands
for hunting boars
and deer. Today's
Boxer was developed
by crossing Danziger
and Brabanter
Bullenbeissers with
other Bavarian and
foreign breeds.

GREAT DANE

The dignified but affectionate Great Dane is the national dog of Germany. Its origins can almost certainly be traced to the dogs brought to Europe by the Alans, a Scythian tribe from what is now Asian Russia. These fighting mastiffs were probably crossed with greyhounds, producing the elegant, distinctive, and gentle breed that exists today. The sheer size of the Great Dane can cause medical problems, including a greater-than-average incidence of hip and elbow arthritis, and bone tumours.

Long, tapering tail is prone to injuries at tip

Short, dense coat covers muscular thighs

KEY FACTS

COUNTRY OF ORIGIN Germany

DATE OF ORIGIN Middle Ages/1800s

FIRST USE War dog, large-mammal hunting

USE TODAY Companion, guarding

LIFE EXPECTANCY 10 years

OTHER NAME German Mastiff

WEIGHT RANGE
46–54 kg (100–120 lb)

HEIGHT RANGE
71–76 cm (28–30 in)

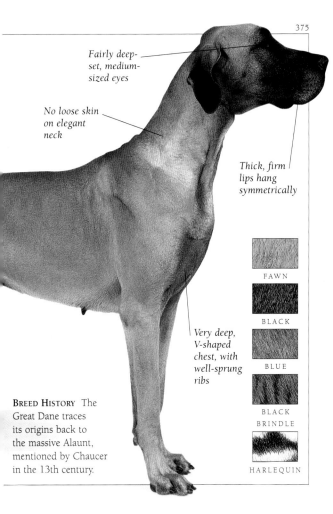

Fairly deep-set, medium-sized eyes

No loose skin on elegant neck

Thick, firm lips hang symmetrically

FAWN

BLACK

BLUE

BLACK BRINDLE

HARLEQUIN

Very deep, V-shaped chest, with well-sprung ribs

BREED HISTORY The Great Dane traces its origins back to the massive Alaunt, mentioned by Chaucer in the 13th century.

SHAR PEI

No other breed in the dog world looks quite like a Shar Pei. Its Chinese standards eloquently describe the breed's conformation – clam-shell ears, butterfly nose, melon-shaped head, grandmotherly face, water-buffalo neck, horse's buttocks, and dragon's legs. The first Shar Peis exported from Hong Kong and bred in the United States had severe eye problems, necessitating repeated surgery. Successive breeding has diminished these conditions, but it has not reduced the very high incidence of skin problems. The Shar Pei can occasionally be aggressive. It is suited to people who are not allergic to dogs, and who are willing to shampoo their dogs frequently.

KEY FACTS

COUNTRY OF ORIGIN China

DATE OF ORIGIN 1500s

FIRST USE Dog fighting, herding, hunting

USE TODAY Companion

LIFE EXPECTANCY 11–12 years

OTHER NAME Chinese Fighting Dog

WEIGHT RANGE
16–20 kg (35–45 lb)

HEIGHT RANGE
46–51 cm (18–20 in)

Head is large
in relation to
size of body

Muzzle is
well padded,
causing bulge
at base of nose

BREED HISTORY A long-time
resident of China's southern
province of Guangdong,
the Shar Pei appears to be
descended from mastiffs
and spitz-type dogs. It is
a fairly close relative of the
Chow Chow. Driven almost
to extinction by China's
prohibition of dogs on the
mainland, the breed was
rescued by Matgo Law,
a Hong Kong breeder.

CREAM

FAWN

RED

BLACK

COMPANION DOGS

ALL DOGS OFFER COMPANIONSHIP, and most look upon the people they live with as members of their own family. Almost all cultures keep pets, usually dogs. Some breeds evolved for no function other than to offer warmth, company, and entertainment. These were generally small dogs, originally created for the amusement of wealthy women.

MINIATURE FORERUNNERS

Dwarfism, where the skull becomes enlarged and domed, and the long bones shorten and the joints thicken, occurred naturally in primitive dogs. These dwarf dogs are the forebears of today's short-legged dachshunds and bassets. Miniaturization (in which all bones are equally reduced in size) also occurred, sometimes along with dwarfism, producing breeds such as the Pekingese, the oldest recognizable companion dog. The Pekingese is probably related to the Shih Tzu and small working dogs such as the Lhasa Apso, Tibetan Terrier, and Tibetan Spaniel, all herders or sentinel dogs. Today, these breeds are sturdy friends, and are increasing in popularity faster than most other companion breeds. The ancient Chinese kept small hairless dogs, both as curiosities and as comforting hot-water bottles.

Shih Tzu

HELD IN HIGH ESTEEM

In Japan, the Japanese Chin became the elite companion of aristocrats, as did the Pekingese in the Chinese royal court, and a miniature spaniel (later named the King Charles) in England. This breed never worked the field, but provided affection and constancy to the king and his favoured friends. Throughout Europe, bichons (small, light-coloured dogs) were the companions of royal courtiers. Close ancestors of the Lowchen, Maltese, Bichon Frise, and Bolognese can be seen in portraits of the ruling classes of Portugal, Spain, France, Italy, and Germany. The Coton de Tulear accompanied the wives of French administrators to Madagascar, while the Havanese became the house pet of wealthy Italians in Argentina and, latterly, Cuba. Chihuahuas are vibrant companions and sentinels, while the larger Pug and French and American Bulldogs are all miniaturized versions of working dogs. So, too, are the Miniature, Toy, and Medium Poodles, kept entirely for companionship, while retaining the trainability of the Standard Poodle. The Dalmatian, originally from a hound background, was subsequently bred for its striking black-spotted coat, and has lost its scent-hunting instincts. Today, its exuberant personality makes it a resourceful, exhilarating companion.

Chihuahua (long-haired variety)

NEW BREEDS AND CROSSES

In North America and the Netherlands, small poodles have been crossed with other breeds to produce popular companion dogs that may soon be recognized as new breeds. Elsewhere, particularly in Australia, the Standard Poodle crossed with the Labrador Retriever is known as the Labradoodle. Some of these cross breeds have non-shedding coats, and have been trained to act as guide dogs for blind people who are allergic to shedding dog hair. The Staffordshire Bull Terrier/Boxer cross is a handsome and rugged dog, while cross breeds of the Bichon Frise and Yorkshire Terrier make sparkling companions. Miniaturization has also created new breeds, such as the Miniature Shar Pei, although some "new" dogs are, in fact, ancient breeds that have never been recognized by kennel clubs. Random-bred dogs, however, remain the world's most popular companions and house dogs.

Bichon Frise

BICHON FRISE

Attractive, adaptable, happy, bold, and lively, the Bichon has found a large following since its emergence from obscurity in the late 1970s. As well as being the ultimate companion dog, this breed is game and hardy – in Norway, farmers recently discovered that it could be trained to round up sheep. Regular grooming is essential. The teeth and gums need attention, since there is a tendency for tartar formation and gum infection. Although many white-haired breeds suffer from chronic skin complaints, the Bichon is relatively free of allergic skin problems.

Hair from tail falls against, but does not press on, back

KEY FACTS

COUNTRY OF ORIGIN Mediterranean region

DATE OF ORIGIN Middle Ages

FIRST USE Companion

USE TODAY Companion

LIFE EXPECTANCY 14 years

OTHER NAME Tenerife Dog

WEIGHT RANGE
3–6 kg (7–12 lb)

HEIGHT RANGE
23–30 cm (9–11 in)

BREED HISTORY
The exact origins of this vivacious and affectionate breed are not known. By the 1300s, sailors had introduced the dog to the island of Tenerife, and by the 15th century it was a royal favourite.

*Jet-black nose
is pink at birth*

*Round, dark
eyes also have
dark rims*

*Drooping
ears are
smaller
than a
poodle's*

*Nails are usually
white, although
breeders prefer black*

MALTESE

Once called the Maltese Terrier, this good-tempered, sweet-natured, sometimes sensitive breed does not shed its hair. It develops a long, luxurious coat, which can become matted, especially at around eight months of age, when the puppy coat is replaced by adult hair. Daily grooming is absolutely essential. The Maltese is almost invariably good with children. It relishes exercise, but when there is no opportunity for this, it will adapt to a more sedentary life.

Weight of long, abundant hair causes tail to curve to side

KEY FACTS

COUNTRY OF ORIGIN Mediterranean region

DATE OF ORIGIN Antiquity

FIRST USE Companion

USE TODAY Companion

LIFE EXPECTANCY 14–15 years

OTHER NAME Bichon Maltaise

WEIGHT RANGE
2–3 kg (4–6 lb)

HEIGHT RANGE
20–25 cm (8–10 in)

BREED HISTORY It is likely that Phoenician traders brought the "Melita" (old term for Malta) breed to Malta over 2,000 years ago. Today's Maltese may be the result of crossing miniature spaniels with the Miniature Poodle.

Large, round, dark eyes

Glossy, heavy coat

BOLOGNESE

The Bolognese closely resembles the Maltese, and served a similar role among the ruling families and aristocracy of Renaissance Italy. Rare today even in Italy, the affectionate Bolognese is slightly more reserved and shy than its more popular cousin, the Bichon Frise. The breed's white, cottony coat makes it suitable for hot climates. The Bolognese enjoys the companionship of people, and forms a close relationship with its owner.

KEY FACTS

COUNTRY OF ORIGIN Italy

DATE OF ORIGIN Middle Ages

FIRST USE Companion

USE TODAY Companion

LIFE EXPECTANCY 14–15 years

OTHER NAME Bichon Bolognese

WEIGHT RANGE
3–4 kg (5–9 lb)

HEIGHT RANGE
25–31 cm (10–12 in)

Small feet, with pink or black nails

BREED HISTORY Although the Bolognese takes its name from the northern Italian city of Bologna, it is possible that the dog is descended from the Bichons of southern Italy. Descriptions of this breed have been recorded since the 1200s.

Hair falls in tufts

Relaxed tail hangs limp; on alert dog, tail curls over back

Legs covered in long hair; dog has no undercoat

HAVANESE

Revolutions are seldom kind to dogs. New regimes often look upon pure-bred dogs as totems of the *ancien régime*. Following the French, Russian, and Cuban revolutions, the cherished breeds of the overthrown classes were actively or passively eliminated. Now rare in Cuba, the Havanese is experiencing a resurgence in popularity in the United States. Sometimes shy, and always gentle and responsive, the Havanese is a natural companion dog, which attaches itself firmly to its human family and is very good with children.

KEY FACTS

COUNTRY OF ORIGIN Mediterranean region/Cuba

DATE OF ORIGIN 1700–1800s

FIRST USE Companion

USE TODAY Companion

LIFE EXPECTANCY 14–15 years

OTHER NAMES Bichon Havanais, Havana Silk Dog

WEIGHT RANGE
3–6 kg (7–13 lb)

HEIGHT RANGE
20–28 cm (8–11 in)

Large, dark eyes covered by hair

Straight legs, with lean toes

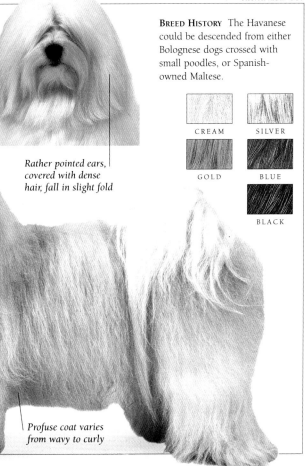

BREED HISTORY The Havanese could be descended from either Bolognese dogs crossed with small poodles, or Spanish-owned Maltese.

CREAM

SILVER

GOLD

BLUE

BLACK

Rather pointed ears, covered with dense hair, fall in slight fold

Profuse coat varies from wavy to curly

COTON DE TULEAR

For centuries, the Coton de Tulear was a favoured companion of the wealthy residents of Tulear, in southern Madagascar, where it continued to breed to type. A dog with similar origins was popular on the French island of Reunion, off the east coast of Madagascar, but became extinct. The Coton, a typical bichon (small, light-coloured companion dog), has a long, fluffy coat that needs careful daily grooming; unlike European bichons, it tends to have patches of yellow or black hair. This gentle, affectionate, and alert breed is becoming increasingly popular in the United States.

KEY FACTS

COUNTRY OF ORIGIN
Madagascar/France

DATE OF ORIGIN 1600s

FIRST USE Companion

USE TODAY Companion

LIFE EXPECTANCY 12–14 years

WEIGHT RANGE
5.5–7 kg (12–15 lb)

HEIGHT RANGE
25–30 cm (10–12 in)

BREED HISTORY Related to
French bichons and the Italian
Bolognese, the Coton possibly
arrived in Madagascar with
French troops, or with the
administrators who followed.
It was virtually unknown
until reintroduced to
Europe and America
in the last 20 years.

WHITE

BLACK/
WHITE

*Long
topcoat;
there is no
undercoat*

*Fluffy hair covers
thin, lightly
muscled forelegs*

LOWCHEN

French in origin, this sparky breed is a true European, with progenitors throughout the countries of southern Europe. Goya is one of many artists to have featured this lively little dog on canvas. Its lion-cut coat makes it look fragile and rather undignified, although this is definitely not the case. The Lowchen is a robust, even tough dog, which can be strong willed and arrogant. Males, in particular, are quite willing to challenge other, larger household dogs for leadership. As in the case of poodles, the breed's hair needs to be clipped only for show purposes.

KEY FACTS

COUNTRY OF ORIGIN France

DATE OF ORIGIN 1600s

FIRST USE Companion

USE TODAY Companion

LIFE EXPECTANCY 12–14 years

OTHER NAME Little Lion Dog

WEIGHT RANGE
4–8 kg (9–18 lb)

HEIGHT RANGE
25–33 cm (10–13 in)

Feet are small and cat-like

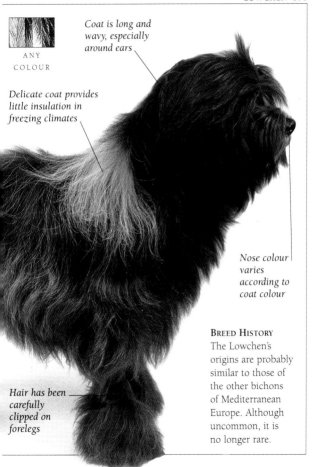

ANY
COLOUR

Coat is long and wavy, especially around ears

Delicate coat provides little insulation in freezing climates

Nose colour varies according to coat colour

Hair has been carefully clipped on forelegs

BREED HISTORY
The Lowchen's origins are probably similar to those of the other bichons of Mediterranean Europe. Although uncommon, it is no longer rare.

LHASA APSO

The Tibetans bred dogs for temperament, not for looks. The Lhasa Apso was used as an indoor sentinel: it would bark aggressively at unfamiliar sounds or sights – its bark is the basis for its Tibetan name, hairy barking dog. Dogs like this were especially popular in the Palace of the Dalai Lama. There was confusion when it was introduced into the West, and it was initially grouped into one category with the Tibetan Terrier and Shih Tzu. In 1934, each of these dogs was recognized as a distinct breed.

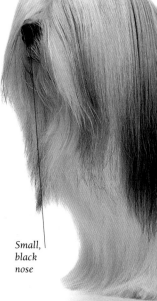

Small, black nose

KEY FACTS

COUNTRY OF ORIGIN Tibet

DATE OF ORIGIN Antiquity

FIRST USE Monks' companion

USE TODAY Companion

LIFE EXPECTANCY 13–14 years

OTHER NAME Apso Seng Kyi

WEIGHT RANGE
6–7 kg (13–15 lb)

HEIGHT RANGE
25–28 cm (10–11 in)

WHITE

BROWN

GOLDEN

BLACK

BICOLOUR

DARK
GRIZZLE

BREED HISTORY For a long
period of time, this breed was
bred exclusively in Tibet. The
first Lhasa Apso arrived in the
West in 1921.

*Coat is heavy
and straight*

SHIH TZU

Although it is very similar in looks to the Lhasa Apso, the Shih Tzu is different in origin and temperament. A translation of the pre-revolutionary Peking Kennel Club's breed standard for the Shih Tzu says it should have "a lion head, bear torso, camel hoof, feather-duster tail, palm-leaf ears, rice teeth, pearly petal tongue, and movement like a goldfish". The Shih Tzu is less aloof and more playful than its Tibetan lookalike, and this probably accounts for its greater worldwide popularity. The hair on the bridge of its nose tends to grow upwards, and is often tied up on the top of the dog's head.

KEY FACTS

COUNTRY OF ORIGIN China

DATE OF ORIGIN 1600s

FIRST USE Emperor's court dog

USE TODAY Companion

LIFE EXPECTANCY 13–14 years

OTHER NAME Chrysanthemum Dog

WEIGHT RANGE
5–7 kg (10–16 lb)

HEIGHT RANGE
25–27 cm (10–11 in)

BREED HISTORY Although the Shih Tzu was bred in the Chinese Royal Court, it is without doubt a cross between Tibetan dogs and ancestors of today's Pekingese.

Tail has natural curl

ANY
COLOUR

Hair on
nose grows
upwards

Black nose is
surrounded
by distinctive
moustache

Long, dense
topcoat

PEKINGESE

According to the rules set by the Chinese Dowager Empress
Tzi Hsi, the Pekingese should have short, bowed legs so
that it cannot wander far, a ruff of fur around its neck to give
it an aura of dignity, and selective taste buds so that it should
appear dainty. She omitted to mention other striking qualities,
including the stubbornness of a mule, the condescension of
the haughty, and the speed of a snail.

The Pekingese is an amusing,
calm, independent dog,
which Chinese legend
says is the result of
a union between a
lion and a monkey,
combining the
nobleness of the
former with
the grace of
the latter.

*Nose is
compressed
flat between
eyes*

*Heavy mane,
and ruff of long,
coarse hair*

BREED HISTORY At one time the exclusive property of the Chinese Royal Courts, and strongly associated with Buddhism, the first four Pekes arrived in the West in 1860.

Profuse double coat conceals bowed legs

KEY FACTS

COUNTRY OF ORIGIN China
DATE OF ORIGIN Antiquity
FIRST USE Companion
USE TODAY Companion
LIFE EXPECTANCY 12–13 years
OTHER NAME Peking Palasthund
WEIGHT RANGE
3–6 kg (7–12 lb)
HEIGHT RANGE
15–23 cm (6–9 in)

ANY
COLOUR

JAPANESE CHIN

British breeders probably crossed this breed with their own toy spaniels, accounting for the similarity between today's Chin and King Charles Spaniel. Like other breeds with flat faces, it can suffer from heart and breathing problems, but the feisty little Chin is independent and robust. As in Japan, where these dogs were owned by noble ladies, Chins also became companions of the wealthy in Europe and America.

KEY FACTS

COUNTRY OF ORIGIN Japan

DATE OF ORIGIN Middle Ages

FIRST USE Companion

USE TODAY Companion

LIFE EXPECTANCY 12 years

OTHER NAMES Japanese Spaniel, Chin

WEIGHT RANGE
2–5 kg (4–11 lb)

HEIGHT RANGE
23–25 cm (9–10 in)

Small, V-shaped ears are carried slightly forwards

BLACK/WHITE   RED/WHITE

BREED HISTORY This breed probably evolved from the Tibetan Spaniel. It first reached Europe in the 1600s, when Portuguese sailors presented some Chins to Princess Catherine of Braganza. Queen Victoria acquired a pair from the American Commodore Perry, after his warships visited Japan.

Large head, with very short, wide, well-cushioned muzzle

Long, straight coat is free from curl

TIBETAN SPANIEL

A spaniel in name only, this breed
never participated in the hunt.
Legend says that in Tibet it was used
as a "prayer dog", trained to turn
the monk's prayer wheel. It has
been a monastery companion
for centuries, and probably
served as a watchdog.
Anatomically similar to the
Pekingese, the leggier, longer
faced Tibetan Spaniel has fewer
breathing or back problems.
Independent and self-confident,
it makes a satisfying companion.

KEY FACTS

COUNTRY OF ORIGIN Tibet

DATE OF ORIGIN Antiquity

FIRST USE Companion in
monasteries

USE TODAY Companion

LIFE EXPECTANCY 13–14 years

WEIGHT RANGE
4–7 kg (9–15 lb)

HEIGHT RANGE
24.5–25.5 cm (10 in)

ANY
COLOUR

*Pendant ears are
feathered with hair
and set quite high*

*Mouth is tipped by
black nose*

BREED HISTORY
Dogs resembling
this breed existed in
the 8th century, in what
is now Korea. Whether
they arrived there from
China or Tibet is unclear.
The Tibetan Spaniel may
be a founder breed of
the Japanese Chin.

TIBETAN TERRIER

The Tibetan Terrier is not a true terrier – it was never bred to go to ground. Historically, it was kept by Tibetan monks for companionship, acting as a very vocal watchdog. Transported to the West by a British medical doctor, Dr. Greig, this alert and inquisitive breed has not attained the popularity of its close relative, the Lhasa Apso. However, it makes a loving companion, requires little exercise, and is reasonably easy to obedience train. Wary of strangers, the Tibetan Terrier has retained its guarding attributes, using its loud voice at the slightest provocation.

Large feet are hidden beneath hair

KEY FACTS

COUNTRY OF ORIGIN Tibet
DATE OF ORIGIN Middle Ages
FIRST USE Guarding
USE TODAY Companion
LIFE EXPECTANCY 13–14 years
OTHER NAME Dhoki Apso
WEIGHT RANGE
8–14 kg (18–30 lb)
HEIGHT RANGE
36–41 cm (14–16 in)

BREED HISTORY The Tibetan Terrier was historically treasured as a gift of tribute. Stories tell that Buddhist monks gave these dogs to nomadic tribes for good luck. The breed was introduced to Great Britain in the 1930s.

Profuse hair on fairly narrow head

Body is compact and powerful

VARIETY
OF
COLOURS

CHINESE CRESTED

The similarities in conformation between the Chinese Crested and hairless African dogs suggest that these breeds might be distantly related. Genetically, hairless dogs do not breed very successfully – they usually have teeth and toenail abnormalities. However, matings between hairless individuals often produce coated puppies, called "powder-puffs". Breeding hairless dogs with powder-puffs, which are genetically more sound, ensures the continuity of this striking breed. The Chinese Crested is lively and affectionate, and makes an affable companion, but it needs to be protected from both hot and cold weather.

POWDER-PUFF VARIETY

While most of body is hairless, tail and ears feature long hair

Chest is well insulated against the elements

Cat-like feet are covered with hair of moderate length

BREED HISTORY Historically, the Chinese are considered to be the most successful "domesticators" of animals, but there is no proof that the Chinese Crested originated in China. Some evidence actually suggests that hairless dogs first developed in Africa, and were then taken by traders to Asia and the Americas.

HAIRLESS VARIETY

VARIETY
OF
COLOURS

Triangular head shape is very similar to that of a Yorkshire Terrier

Lean, elegant build

Plain or spotted skin lightens in summer

KEY FACTS

COUNTRY OF ORIGIN China/Africa

DATE OF ORIGIN Antiquity

FIRST USE Companion/comforter

USE TODAY Companion

LIFE EXPECTANCY 12–13 years

OTHER NAMES Hairless, Powder-puff

WEIGHT RANGE
2–5.5 kg (5–12 lb)

HEIGHT RANGE
23–33 cm (9–13 in)

PUG

Pugs are an acquired habit, but they become addictive. Pugnacious and individualistic, this vibrant breed is extremely tough and opinionated. It is independent and resolute – it knows what it wants and stands its ground. The Pug's compact, muscular body, flat face, and unblinking stare give it a strong presence and personality. Yet although strong willed and forceful, it is rarely aggressive. Affectionate with its human family, the breed makes an amusing and rewarding companion.

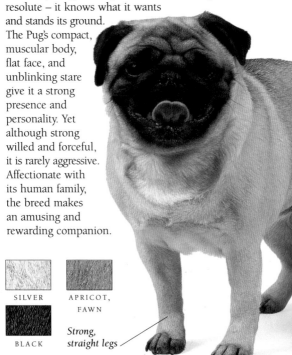

SILVER

APRICOT, FAWN

BLACK

Strong, straight legs

BREED HISTORY Miniaturized from mastiffs in the Far East at least 2,400 years ago, the Pug's ancestors were once companions of Buddhist priests. Introduced into Holland in the 1500s via the Dutch East India Company, this dog then became the companion of aristocrats and kings.

KEY FACTS

COUNTRY OF ORIGIN China

DATE OF ORIGIN Antiquity

FIRST USE Companion

USE TODAY Companion

LIFE EXPECTANCY 13–15 years

OTHER NAMES Carlin, Mops

WEIGHT RANGE
6–8 kg (14–18 lb)

HEIGHT RANGE
25–28 cm (10–11 in)

Tightly curled, twisted tail

Thin, soft, small, velvety, high-set ears

Smooth coat is neither hard nor woolly

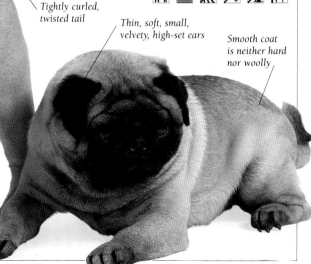

KING CHARLES SPANIEL

Reports by Samuel Pepys and other British diarists tell that King Charles II seemingly spent more time with his spaniels than with affairs of state. His dogs were larger and had longer noses than today's breed, but in accordance with fashion, both the dog and its nose gradually shrank to the present proportions. It is possible that crosses with the Japanese Chin helped to bring about these changes. Delightfully affectionate, the breed makes a superb urban companion.

KEY FACTS

COUNTRY OF ORIGIN Great Britain

DATE OF ORIGIN 1600s

FIRST USE Companion

USE TODAY Companion

LIFE EXPECTANCY 12 years

OTHER NAME English Toy Spaniel

WEIGHT RANGE
4–6 kg (8–14 lb)

HEIGHT RANGE
25–27 cm (10–11 in)

Long, silky coat can be straight or wavy

BLENHEIM   TRICOLOUR   BLACK/
TAN

RED/TAN

*Low-set ears hang
flat to cheeks*

BREED HISTORY
By the 1600s,
selective breeding of the
smallest spaniels from single
litters had produced
a "toy" spaniel, later named
after King Charles II, one of
its most obsessive admirers.

*Straight legs,
with compact,
well-fringed feet*

CAVALIER KING CHARLES SPANIEL

A success story of recent years, the friendly, affable, and energetic Cavalier has become very popular. In many ways it is an ideal urban canine companion, willing to curl up on a sofa in bad weather, but equally willing to walk and run for miles. Unfortunately, the breed's growing popularity has led to intensive in-breeding, which has contributed to an overwhelming increase in lethal heart conditions. The consequence is that the life expectancy of affected dogs is reduced from 14 to only nine or 10 years. This is perhaps the highest incidence of any serious inherited disease in any breed. When selecting one of these dogs, it is extremely important to check the medical history of several previous generations.

BLENHEIM

RUBY

BLACK/
TAN

TRICOLOUR

BREED HISTORY In the 1920s, an American, Roswell Eldridge, offered prize money at Cruft's Dog Show in London to anyone exhibiting King Charles Spaniels with long noses, as depicted in Van Dyck's painting of King Charles II and his spaniels. By the 1940s, these dogs were classified as a unique breed and given the prefix Cavalier, to set them apart from their forebears.

KEY FACTS

COUNTRY OF ORIGIN Great Britain
DATE OF ORIGIN 1925
FIRST USE Companion
USE TODAY Companion
LIFE EXPECTANCY 10–14 years
WEIGHT RANGE
5–8 kg (10–18 lb)
HEIGHT RANGE
31–33 cm (12–13 in)

Moderately muscled thighs, with solid bone

Feathering of hair along straight, well-boned forelegs

Long, silky coat has slight wave, but no curl

CHIHUAHUA

Although small and fragile, the Chihuahua is alert and bold. It is named after the Mexican state from which it was first exported to the United States. Legends surround the breed; its Aztec name, Xoloitzcuintli, appears to be a misnomer – this was another, much larger, Central American animal. Other legends, declaring that blue-coated dogs were sacred and red-coated ones were ritually sacrificed, are also dubious. Certainly, the Chihuahua is the ultimate toy lapdog. Shivering at the slightest breeze, and most content on the lap of its human companion, both the short-haired and better insulated long-haired varieties offer good humour, comfort, constancy, and companionship.

Long-haired variety has large ruff of top hair, with full undercoat around neck

Small feet have very curved nails

BREED HISTORY The origins of the Chihuahua are shrouded in mystery. Experts speculate that small dogs arrived in the Americas with the Spanish armies of Hernando Cortes in 1519. Another theory is that the Chinese voyaged to America, bringing with them miniaturized dogs before the arrival of Europeans. The Chihuahua was first exported to the United States in the 1850s.

KEY FACTS

COUNTRY OF ORIGIN Mexico

DATE OF ORIGIN 1800s?

FIRST USE Companion

USE TODAY Companion

LIFE EXPECTANCY 12–14 years

WEIGHT RANGE
1–3 kg (2–6 lb)

HEIGHT RANGE
15–23 cm (6–9 in)

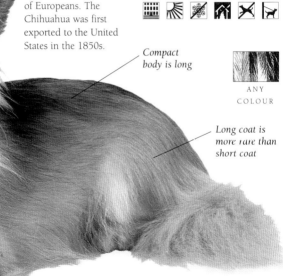

Compact body is long

ANY
COLOUR

Long coat is more rare than short coat

FRENCH BULLDOG

Although stories persist that the French Bulldog descends from a Spanish bull baiter (the Dogue de Burgos), there is convincing evidence that this often opinionated little dog descends from "miniature" Bulldogs produced in Great Britain. Curiously, the French Bulldog was first recognized as a distinct breed not in France or Great Britain, but in the United States. Originally bred for the utilitarian purpose of tenacious ratting, this muscular companion then became the fashion accessory of working-class Paris. No longer as numerous as it once was, the French Bulldog has moved up the social ladder and now resides in more affluent households.

KEY FACTS

COUNTRY OF ORIGIN France

DATE OF ORIGIN 1800s

FIRST USE Bull baiting

USE TODAY Companion

LIFE EXPECTANCY 11–12 years

OTHER NAME Bouledogue Français

WEIGHT RANGE
10–13 kg (22–28 lb)

HEIGHT RANGE
30.5–31.5 cm (12 in)

FAWN

PIED

RED
BRINDLE

BLACK
BRINDLE

BREED HISTORY In the 1860s, French dog breeders imported some very small Bulldogs from Great Britain and bred them with French terriers. By the 1900s, the French Bulldog was popular in Paris as a butcher's and coachman's companion.

Broad, short, snub nose has slanting nostrils

Ears cropped for fashion purposes only

Cylindrical, barrel-like rib cage

Very short, thick, glossy, soft coat

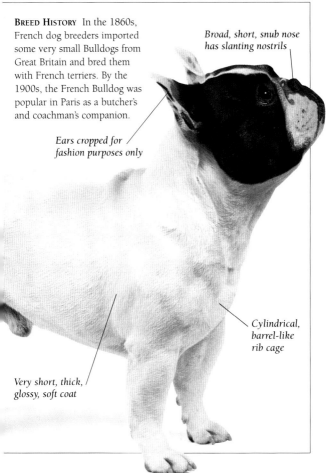

POODLES

Fifty years ago, the poodle was the world's most popular dog – a fashion accessory in cities worldwide. With popularity, however, came indiscriminate breeding for quantity, not quality. Both physical and behavioural problems crept into this alert and highly trainable breed, and it fell from favour. Today, safe in the hands of knowledgeable breeders, small poodles are once more reliable companions. Miniaturization sometimes brings with it a heightened puppy-like dependence upon people, but in the case of poodles, sound individuals retain powerfully independent personalities. At their best, these dogs are exceptionally responsive, trainable, and thoughtful.

KEY FACTS

COUNTRY OF ORIGIN France

DATE OF ORIGIN 1500s

FIRST USE Companion

USE TODAY Companion

LIFE EXPECTANCY 14–17 years

OTHER NAME Caniche

WEIGHT RANGE
Toy: 6.5–7.5 kg (14–16½ lb)
Miniature: 12–14 kg (26–30 lb)
Medium: 15–19 kg (33–42 lb)

HEIGHT RANGE
Toy: 25–28 cm (10–11 in)
Miniature: 28–38 cm (11–15 in)
Medium: 34–38 cm (13–15 in)

BREED HISTORY Herd-guarding and water-retrieving Standard Poodles were probably taken from Germany to France at least 500 years ago. Certainly by that time, the poodle had been "bantomized" to the reduced size of today's Toy Poodle.

ALL
SOLID
COLOURS

TOY POODLE

Ears are covered with wavy hair

Muzzle is straight

BREED HISTORY A miniaturized version of the Standard Poodle, the Miniature Poodle became extremely popular during the 1950s and 1960s. Slightly larger than the Toy Poodle, this agile breed was once a regular performer in the circus ring.

MINIATURE POODLE

Woolly, springy coat

Pom-poms on hind legs give clown effect

Small, oval feet; nails vary with coat colour

BREED HISTORY Although not formally recognized everywhere, the Medium Poodle, sized midway between the Miniature and Standard, is accepted in some countries as a separate breed.

MEDIUM
POODLE

Lively eyes are slightly slanted

Resilient, curly, non-shedding hair needs frequent trimming

Hair is left uncut on tail tip

Forelegs are straight and parallel

DALMATIAN

Although today the Dalmatian breed is kept solely as a companion, for centuries it was a superb working dog. In its time it has been a pack hunter, a retriever, and a bird dog. It has been used to herd sheep and catch vermin. More recently, it has been used as a circus performer. Until the advent of motorized transportation, the Dalmatian was used as a carriage dog. Uniquely among all breeds, it would walk alongside horse-drawn carriages, clearing the road ahead in populated areas. In the 1800s, American fire departments used it to control the horses that pulled fire appliances. Today, this exuberant dog serves as a companion. Almost invariably friendly, some males can be aggressive to other male dogs. The Dalmatian is the only breed of dog that can suffer from urate stones in its urinary system.

WHITE/
LIVER

WHITE/
BLACK

Thighs are round and muscular

Tail is strong at root, tapering to tip

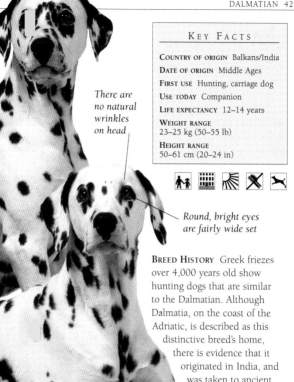

There are no natural wrinkles on head

Round, bright eyes are fairly wide set

BREED HISTORY Greek friezes over 4,000 years old show hunting dogs that are similar to the Dalmatian. Although Dalmatia, on the coast of the Adriatic, is described as this distinctive breed's home, there is evidence that it originated in India, and was taken to ancient Greece by traders.

RANDOM-BRED DOGS

REFERRED TO AS MONGRELS, random-bred dogs all share one characteristic. Since they were not bred for an exclusive purpose, they are far less likely to suffer from inherited medical problems such as blindness, heart disease, and hip dysplasia that occur with distressing frequency in certain pure-bred dogs. Although random-bred dogs are plentiful and inexpensive to buy, the companionship they provide is no less rewarding.

INFLUENCES ON PERSONALITY

A dog's personality is determined by many factors, the most important being genetics and early environment. Genetics are profoundly influential – breeding dogs of similar temperament is more likely to produce dogs of like disposition than breeding dogs with disparate characters. This, of course, is the basis of selective breeding – by choosing a specific breed, it is more likely that you will acquire a dog with known behaviour traits than if you choose a random-bred dog. Genetics, however, do not determine the whole personality. Early environment is very critical. Random-bred puppies raised properly in a family environment grow to become reliable adults. Unfortunately, random-bred dogs are often the results of unplanned pregnancies, and owners sometimes disregard or even discard them. These dogs consistently show a high level of anxiety-related behaviour problems.

FERAL DOGS

Feral dogs are random bred; they eat, breed, give birth, and survive outside homes, but depend upon the detritus of human habitation for survival. Although few feral dogs exist in North America and northern Europe, they are common in Central and South America, in parts of the Balkans and the former Soviet empire, in Turkey

Alert guardian

Robust cross breed

and the Middle East, and in Africa and Asia. They breed randomly, yet often true to type – if their breeding were brought under human control, regional random-bred dogs would be reclassified into pure-bred categories.

Acquiring a random-bred dog

The best way to acquire a random-bred dog is from a neighbour or a friend's litter of puppies, so that the mother's temperament, and ideally also the father's, can be observed. Choosing a puppy removes unknown variables of early learning that can dramatically affect later temperament.

In dog shelters, there is always a surplus of random-bred dogs in need of good homes. Some of these, rescued by organizations producing assistance dogs for the disabled, have been successfully trained in obedience and complicated sound-response skills. Eventual adult size can be difficult

to estimate with some random-bred puppies, and can vary dramatically among members of the same litter. So, too, can coat length and texture.

Temperament testing

Dogs from rescue centres have more temperament and behaviour problems than those kept in stable households. Some shelters test character; potential owners can also pose relevant mock scenarios to assess a dog's personality. However, in its ability to offer companionship and affection, or to bark a warning against intruders, the random-bred dog is generally as efficient as any pure breed. In its sheer doggedness, nothing outshines it.

Loyal companions

INDEX

A

B

C

D

ACKNOWLEDGMENTS

PUBLISHER'S ACKNOWLEDGMENTS
Dorling Kindersley would like to thank photographer Tracy Morgan for her invaluable contribution to *Dogs*, as well as the many dog owners who allowed their dogs to be photographed. Thanks also to Tim Scott and Heather McCarry for design assistance, Jane Bolton for editorial assistance, Margaret McCormack for compiling the index, and Bob Gordon and Helen Parker at PAGE*One* for initial design and editorial work.

PHOTOGRAPHIC CREDITS
KEY: l = left, r = right, t = top, b = bottom, c = centre
All photography by Tracy Morgan except:
L. Gardiner: 72–73; D. King: 18–19, 29t, 192b, 345t, 423b; T. Ridley: 422; D. Ward: 423t